GRANVILLE
A MOTHER'S GRIEF

JUNE OLLERENSHAW

First published in 2011.

National Library of Australia Cataloguing-in-Publication entry:

Author: Ollerenshaw, June

Title: Granville : a mother's grief / June Ollerenshaw

Edition: 2nd

ISBN: 9781921555985 (pbk.)

Subjects: Ollerenshaw, June.
Ollerenshaw, Cathy.
Ollerenshaw, Lyndy.
Mothers and daughters--Biography.
Grief--Personal narratives.
Loss (Psychology)
Granville Rail Disaster, 1977.

Dewey Number: 155.93

Typeset in Minion Pro.

Published by Boolarong Press, Salisbury, Brisbane, Australia.

Printed and bound by Watson Ferguson & Company, Salisbury, Brisbane, Australia.

No Tomorrows

The death of a child is like a permanent bruise
on the heart.

The death of two children is like your heart has
been torn apart.

How could such pain ever go away?

Over the years many people have said such things as:

You have to get over it.

You should be over it by now.

You must pull yourself together.

You just have to get on with your life.

No-one ever could teach me how.

Acknowledgements

My sincere thanks to all those friends who have encouraged me over the 11 years I have spent writing this book.

First and foremost Carolyn Laird. Carolyn gave me a year of her time and energy. She continually encouraged me with her enthusiasm and fresh ideas, improving on what I was attempting to do. I feel emotional about the effect I believe the book and the work she did with me had on her life. I believe the book has changed Carolyn to a degree in the way she now looks at life and her values as a Mother. Thank you my dear friend. You are one of God's special people.

Thank you to the other friends who so willingly read my manuscript and encouraged me in the early days of this momentous project. Erika Denning, Patricia Brookman, and Christine Carr. Beverley Sines for her input. Anna Kassulke who did the early editing… thank you.

My sincere thanks especially to Stephen Cain my son-in-law, for allowing me to tell his story to the world.

To my editor Shannon Ryan I have been privileged to have him in my life. His encouragement and enthusiasm were uplifting and exciting.

My publisher Dan Kelly thank you for you unstinting support.

Chapter Titles

DEDICATION

This book is dedicated to the memory of my two darling daughters, Cathy and Lyndy.

Both my girls died in the Granville Train Disaster on 18th January, 1977.

CHAPTER 1

RUNNING FOR THE TRAIN

18th January 1977. As the hot summer sun rose high in the sky, people all over Sydney were waking up and preparing for another day. The air felt warm, and even though it was only seven in the morning there was already the promise of another balmy January day ahead. Cathy Cain began the day in her usual way. At just 19 years of age, Cathy was already married and living with her husband, Stephen, in a small suburban house in Parramatta. As Cathy dressed in her official bank uniform and brushed her long, blonde hair she wondered optimistically what the day would bring. She caught a glimpse of her reflection in the mirror and saw a pretty and petite young woman looking back at her. Even though she was only five foot tall her big blue eyes and bubbly personality more than made up for her height. She hummed happily to herself as she sat down to a quick breakfast of toast and coffee and skimmed the headlines of the morning paper. Sambo, her beloved Alsatian cross, was always by her side, and this morning he lay sprawled out under her feet waiting for any titbits she might throw his way. Instead, she gave him a huge hug, put him outside in the back yard and waved him goodbye before leaving the house at the usual time of 7.45am.

Cathy set out on foot for Parramatta Railway Station where she would meet her sister, Lyndy, and Lyndy's best friend, Angela, and travel with them to the city. All three girls worked at banks in the city. Cathy and Lyndy both worked for the CBC Bank in George Street, Martin Place, Sydney, while Angela worked nearby in the ANZ Bank. Cathy didn't have to rush to get to the station this morning.

She was in plenty of time to meet her travelling companions, and as she leisurely made her way down Victoria Road, her long, blonde hair streaming down her back, she let her thoughts linger on the plans she was making for her first wedding anniversary. Just two nights ago she had spoken to her mum about what they would do and where they would go. She didn't really care what they ended up doing as long as they were together. The day Cathy married Stephen had been the happiest day of her life and now almost a year had passed. She couldn't quite believe it, the time had flown, and as she thought about their year together she knew she loved him more now than ever.

A dog barking somewhere behind her interrupted Cathy's thoughts, and when she turned to see where the barking was coming from she saw Sambo running towards her.

"Sambo," she cried out, "what are you doing here?" and she bent down and gave him a quick hug. "Come on, back home for you," she said as she led her dog home.

By the time she had gotten Sambo home and made sure he was locked safely in the back yard 10 minutes had slipped by. Cathy glanced at her watch in desperation and saw that she was now running very late for her usual train, the 6.09am commuter train from the Blue Mountains.

Cathy began to run as fast as she could up Victoria Road

towards the station. An elderly lady who lived across the road saw her and waved, but Cathy did not have time to stop so she gave a quick wave back and continued on her way.

Every now and again she would glance down at her watch and then run a little faster, willing her legs to move more quickly so she would make the train. She knew that Lyndy and Angela would be waiting on the train for her as they usually did, and she didn't want to miss seeing them as they always travelled together – always on the 6.09am from the Blue Mountains – always the second carriage.

Cathy turned left into Church Street and then left again into Darcy Street, and as she rounded the corner she could see the train slowing down to stop at the station. Already panting and perspiring in the January heat, she pushed herself to keep running, and as she flew up the ramp to the platform she saw that the train had now stopped in the station. Lyndy and Angela had stepped off the train and were standing on the platform waiting for her. She saw them as they saw her and they all smiled and waved madly at each other. Lyndy and Angela ran up the platform to meet Cathy, and because the train was just about to pull out they all jumped quickly into the nearest carriage – the fourth carriage. They were just in time. The doors slammed shut and the train jerked forward and pulled noisily out from the station, throwing the girls off balance. The three girls jostled forward unsteadily to find a seat where they could sit together, and when they finally sat down, Cathy let out a sigh of relief – she had made the train.

From the coroner's finding:

At 8.12am on 18th January, 1977, the locomotive 4620 of the passenger train 108 was derailed while negotiating a left-hand curve, travelling east on the up lane western line near the Granville Railway Station. As a result of this derailment, the locomotive came into collision with the northern trestle supporting the upper decking of the Bold Street Bridge. It continued on demolishing the eight steel stanchions of that trestle, coming to rest on its right-hand side, 220 feet further on. A steel electric power line was sheared off its base and this mast suspended by overhead electrical wires collided with and demolished carriage number one . Carriage number two suffered little damage and came to rest clear of the bridge. When the train came to rest, the rear and leading ends of carriages three and four respectively came to rest under the Bold Street Bridge. At this point in time the bridge collapsed on to these three carriages. Deaths occurred in carriages one, three and four, totalling 83.

CHAPTER 2

A PERFECT EXAMPLE OF A HUMAN BEING

DOROTHY: 23rd September 1908–6th May, 1966

My precious mother, Dorothy, had a weak heart. It was the result of contracting rheumatic fever (rheumatic carditis) when she was seven years old. She had never gone out to work as such, but she was very gifted with her hands. In the days of the glory box she would needlework a whole trousseau for family and friends. I still, to this day, have pieces of her work around me in every room of my home. I always saw her as a big woman with a very big heart. Sadly, to my knowledge, my elder daughter, Cathy, was the only one of her eight granddaughters who inherited her gift for fine needlework.

It was the spring of 1936; Dorothy was heavily pregnant with her second child. She had just nine weeks to go. At the time the family was living in Margaret Street, Granville, NSW. It was September 18th and the August winds were still around. Like most people, Dorothy was heartily sick of the "westerlies."

Her young son Jack, (John Victor), five years old at the time, was playing in the garden. It was about 3.30 in the afternoon and Dorothy was cooking the vegetables for dinner on the gas cooker. She thought she would take advantage of the early start she had made on dinner and lie down to rest for 15 minutes. However, when her head hit the pillow she quickly fell into a deep sleep. Quite some time later she woke up with a start.

"Oh, dear God," she shouted. "I can smell smoke! The house must be on fire!"

She ran as quickly as she could to the kitchen and saw to her horror that the lace curtains over the stove were on fire.

Immediately, she ran to the garden to get the hose. Dorothy, being the strong-minded, level-headed person she was, put out the flames, seemingly with little fuss.

But, possibly due to her heart condition, she was overcome by smoke and fell unconscious to the kitchen floor, her hands covering her face.

Her sister, Ella, arrived soon after for her routine check on her sister. To her horror, she found Dorothy on the kitchen floor in a pool of blood. Immediately she realised that I, June Dorothy, had made a premature and dramatic entrance into this world, right there on the kitchen floor. Ella saw the tiny baby lying in a pool of blood and flew into emergency mode. So there I was: a tiny being, barely alive, struggling to take my first breath, still attached to my mother by the umbilical cord. In all my years I have always held the notion that this cord has never really been severed.

As Ella looked at my tiny body she was overcome with sadness when she discovered the purple imprint of my mother's hands on my tiny face. Even as she arranged for an ambulance, she prayed "Oh please God, don't let my tiny niece be marked for life."

Dad (Victor), Aunty Madge (Mum's older sister) and the ambulance all arrived at the same time. Naturally, they all wanted to travel in the ambulance with the tiny baby that was me to the Tresillian at Vaucluse House, Vaucluse which was a long way away from Granville in the western suburbs of Sydney.

Ella said emphatically, "I'm going. I'm closest to Dot." Madge persisted, "I should go. I'm the eldest." My Dad shouted, "Well I'm going. She's my little daughter."

Then the ambulance man said, "If you don't make up your bloody minds, I'll go without the lot of you!" In the end, Dad and Madge won out.

Madge nursed me in the ambulance for what she was sure would be my first and last trip through the streets of Sydney. Dad sat opposite feeling anxious.

Finally, we set off, down Margaret Street, out on to Railway Parade and then Parramatta Road, with all the sirens blazing, on our way to the Tresillian at Vaucluse – a hospital for premature babies. As we were driving through Granville, Madge was pessimistic about my chances. "Not much hope for this little one," she thought. "All they can do is wrap her in cotton wool and put her in a shoe box." There weren't any incubators in those days, and not too many of the "premmie" babies survived.

About halfway to the hospital, I breathed a deep sigh. Madge cried, "Vic, I think she has just breathed her last."

Dad was agitated, "No way Madge, she's my darling daughter. I know she will survive."

With love like that I believe I had to survive.

Back at Margaret Street, Ella called in the family G.P, Doctor Stanton, who insisted Dorothy should go to hospital at once. She flatly refused to leave her young son Jack and so Doctor Stanton attended to her daily at home to monitor her heart.

So began my struggle to live. I was and always have been a survivor. I have often felt that my tough, against-all-odds beginning prepared me for the many battles that life held in store for me.

I was christened June Dorothy, and although I had made my dramatic entrance into the world weighing in at 3 pounds, I quickly lost 13 ounces within the first week.

My dad journeyed with a flask of expressed breast milk by train every day into Wynyard Railway Station, and then he walked to Circular Quay, where he caught the ferry to Vaucluse. Then he reversed the journey to return home. This went on for six weeks. However, it was a labour of love. Victor had the beloved daughter he had always wanted and he was not going to give me up. I was his treasure and remained his treasure always.

Finally, I came home from hospital. Mum carried me on a pillow for six months. I was too tiny to handle, she said.

And then, because it looked as if I was born with the imprint of my mother's hands on my tiny face in purple birthmarks, Mum took me to the convent to see the nuns. She had incredible faith in spiritual healing. They bathed my face in holy water, and after a few months the purple birthmarks had faded away. The story of my miraculous recovery was told around the streets of Granville for many years after.

There had always been a special bond between Mum and me. She had delivered me alone without the help of a doctor. There had not been anyone to smack my bottom to make me take my first breath. Many times throughout my life it came down to just her and me. She was always wonderfully supportive of me any time I came up against trouble or tragedy. She was always so calm and seemed able to take anything that life threw her way in her stride.

Dad, on the other hand, was ecstatic. He had the daughter he longed for, his little treasure.

Mum had been told she would never carry another child after my birth. However, she went on to have a third child, Kenneth Rupert, five years later.

CHAPTER 3

WALLACE STREET, GRANVILLE

We were a working-class family living in Granville in the western suburbs of Sydney. I lived in Granville from 1936 until 1956, and I never really moved more than a few kilometres away until I moved to Perth in about 1979.

Granville in those days was a working-class suburb. It was a decent place to live and rear a family. The Commonwealth Bank took up a stately position on the corner of Railway Parade and Bold Street. It was the only bank in our suburb. There were two hotels, a swimming pool, a library and a block of shops. The Granville Railway Station sat in the middle of the town. There was an overhead walking bridge across the railway line. The Bold Street Bridge was constructed some years later. Saint Mark's Church sat in behind the shops. It is the oldest church in Australia. The important place for me was the one milk bar in town. It was here where we all met up for milkshakes. I was forbidden to go near this bad place, as my mother called it. I often popped in to meet up with my friends. I lived in horror of Mum finding out.

I was born in Margaret Street and when I was two years old my parents won a major prize in the NSW State lottery. This meant that my mum and dad were able to purchase their own home at No. 1 Wallace Street, Granville.

Number 1 was a two-bedroom weatherboard construction, with a kitchen, bathroom, lounge, sleep-out, a hall with a wonderful red carpet, a laundry in the house and yes, an indoor loo! We really had moved up in the world. It also had a small brick, semi-enclosed front patio. This was one of my favourite places. I loved to play there. Whenever we had an electric storm Mum would take us all out on to the patio to watch the thunder and lightning. I still love to watch thunder and lightning. My mum was not a great one for instilling fear into her children.

When I was five years old my brother, Kenneth Rupert, was born. Even though I don't recollect starting school, I do remember vividly Ken being born. I adored him. Mum would sit me on the kitchen floor, nursing Ken between my legs, so I could give him his bottle of milk. I remember when Ken was circumcised I asked Mum why he was bleeding. She said when the doctor brought him to us in his bag the bag closed on his tummy, making him bleed. My little world was complete. Even at such a tender age, I had great maternal instincts.

My Aunt Ella, who lived nearby, had two children my age Patty and Max, and then she had like a second family of three boys, Michael, Johnny and Robert. My Aunt Ella, or Lullie as I always called her, would allow me to push her babies in the pram up to the Granville shops. I would have only been about 12 years old at the time and a very small child.

My mum would never have approved of this, so I had to keep it a secret. These two sisters were entirely different. That was a special time for me, in my own little world, playing mother.

Mum was often ill. She had several strokes when I was a child, but even so she would never have anyone do her housework or cooking.

My parents never laid a hand on me in anger. However, the boys were always in trouble. My older brother, Jack, in particular, was always in strife. I adored him in those days. He was my knight in shining armour. I always saw him as a handsome, debonair boy. Always whistling and happy, he had an air of bravado about him and was very protective of me. When his mates came to stay they would not dare to swear in front of me. But Jack was a terrible torment; especially to my younger brother, Ken, he tormented him mercilessly. I was always amazed at him because he would laugh while Ken would be crying. I would be worried and Jack would laugh and laugh.

I can still see Mum chasing Jack around the garden with the strap. Fortunately, she didn't catch him too often. I was always praying he would escape.

After one of these outbursts Jack would disappear for a couple of hours. Next thing, he would come through the back door, whistling away, and nothing more would be said about the incident. Mum had calmed down, was obviously over it. He could read her well, maybe she didn't really want to catch him. He had us all thoroughly charmed.

Every Christmas, Jack would tell me about this wonderful present he had for me. He would have me guessing for weeks, nearly sick with anticipation. I remember one year he made a mat for my bedroom out of bottle tops.

It was grotesque! He thought it was great. I managed to smile sweetly and tell him I loved it. Another time, in 1944, he gave me a biro. Great, this was something I could use. None of my friends had seen a biro before. It was unique. That Christmas I was thoroughly impressed.

One year our next-door neighbours, the Crouchs, bought a pig to fatten for all our Christmas dinners. We named him Rupert and we all became thoroughly attached. Come Christmas, poor Rupert was sent to the chopping block. He was to be shared between the three neighbouring families.

Mr Crouch was given the task of chief-beheader.

As he raised the axe, all of the kids started to cry, crying for him to stop. This apparently unnerved poor Mr Crouch and he burst into tears. He dropped the axe and walked away. Rupert's execution was deferred for now.

We never ever found out who eventually did the dirty on Rupert. Of course my dad was under heavy suspicion for a long time. At the long-awaited Christmas dinner, no-one, including Dad or Mr Crouch, could bring themselves to eat Rupert. Mum hated to waste food, so she donated him to the nuns at the local convent.

I remember that Mum had a terrible temper. She had been asking Dad to put a window in the kitchenette for ages. She was a great cook and always baking, and the little room was extremely hot in summer. Mum kept on nagging Dad for this window, but it was falling on deaf ears. Then one day she must have just lost control. She went to the garage and found the axe. Mum used the axe to physically chop a great hole in the back wall!

Now Dad, being a proud man, was furious at her outrageous behaviour. Everything had to be neat and tidy in and around our home. Mum had her large window installed within the week.

Our family went on holidays for two weeks most summers. We travelled by train; it took 20 hours in those days to the north coast of NSW to Sawtell or Nambucca Heads. As a child, I just loved that 20-hour journey. I was fascinated with the large bottles of water with the silver lids hanging on a chain attached to the wall, the seat that folded away so people could go to the toilet and the small fold-down table. I thought the whole journey was wonderful. One of us children would want a drink every 10 minutes, until Dad eventually got sick of jumping up and down.

Finally, to Dad's great relief, we would arrive at our destination, a holiday house by the sea at Urunga or Sawtell.

Mum's first job was to pull all the mattresses off the beds, put them in the sun, and disinfect the bed bases. None of the family ever questioned this. Looking back, it was a wonder she ever left home with all the work she created for herself. To me it seems a long way to go to wash beds.

We had a good life as children. Dad took us on excursions to the city of Sydney–always on Sundays. We visited places such as the Art Gallery, the Museum, and the Botanical Gardens.

The place I liked best was Manly Beach with the tall Norfolk Island palms and ice creams on the Esplanade. We always had a walk past the "Far West Children's Home" and Dad would relate to us about the little children who were brought there for a holiday from out west and how some of them had never seen the ocean in their lives before. Sometimes, he told us these children were even afraid of the ocean when they first saw it. I can still remember being amazed that anyone could be afraid of the sea.

When I was about seven years old, we had visitors. Because there were not enough chairs to seat everybody, Dad brought my little green table into the house for me to sit on. Unfortunately for me, there was a Redback spider under the table and I was bitten. Someone ran for a neighbour, Mrs Walker, the local bag merchant's wife, who was a nursing sister. She sucked the poison out of my leg before I was taken to Parramatta Hospital. I survived and Mum remarked that Mrs Walker obviously has no cavities in her teeth or she would have been dead, poisoned.

This experience left an impression on me. I still to this day check under outdoor chairs before I sit on them. I remember as a child, I always thought "Mrs Walker could have died." It seems to me that parents often forget how a chance remark can worry small children and leave a lasting impression on them.

As a small child I would lie in bed of a night and listen to the hum of my parents talking in bed, and it was always a comfort to listen to the sound of their voices as I drifted off to sleep. As I got older I began to think how romantic it was as I lay there listening to the beautiful sounds of two people talking until they finally slept.

My mum and I, seven months old.

CHAPTER 4

TEENAGE YEARS

In August 1951, I was almost 15 years old. I had been menstruating for two years and always suffered incredible pain at that time every month. I had been ill for several days and finally I was rushed to hospital. They were treating me for colic. I can still remember the excruciating pain. I could not bear anyone leaning on the bed. It was the end of the day and Doctor Newton, a Macquarie Street specialist, had been operating at the hospital all day. He was ready to go home when one of the nuns said to him, "Doctor, we have a child here, sick with colic. Could you have a look at her?" Well, from there it was all systems go. Dr Newton decided to operate at once. I had a diseased tube and ovary removed. He would not wait for parental consent. Mum and Dad were outside the front doors of the hospital waiting for visiting hours to commence. They had no idea of the emergency going on inside. Then their names were called. Dr Newton hadn't waited. He had me in the operating theatre undergoing surgery. He told me some time later if I had not been in a Catholic hospital he would have performed a full hysterectomy. He also added, "June, my dear, you will never carry a child."

I have never forgotten the day I came home from hospital. Dad said to me, "Look at the garden, darling. The portulacas are all out in flower, all smiling, to welcome you home." It was my 15th birthday. There has seldom been a summer when I have not had them growing in my garden. Looking out the window, writing this, I can see my two large beds of portulacas.

Even back then, I knew I wanted five children, starting with twin boys. I never got my twin boys or my five children.

One of Mum's sisters was a shocking gossip. The word spread around Granville very smartly, "Little Junee Ollerenshaw will never be able to have children." Of course I soon heard the gossip. I was devastated!

A couple of years later I took myself off to Macquarie Street to see Dr Newton again. Yes, he reinformed me, I would never become pregnant.

I was shattered. I walked along Macquarie Street with my head down feeling it was the end of the world. No children, ever, how could that be!

I had always been a "doll" person. This carried over to my baby brother, to my Aunty Ella's babies, pushing them around the streets, and now, at such a tender age, to be told "no children."

Aunt Ella's second youngest son, Johnny, was the apple of my Mum's eye. She adored him. He started school when he was five years old, but loathed it. Johnny had to pass our house on the way to school. Mum told me later, many a morning Johnny would call in to her and say he felt sick. She always kept him home from school. Then Ella would come down later in the morning for a cuppa, which was her normal routine if Dot did not go up to her. She told me she always hid Johnny in the bedroom until his mother had gone home.

One Sunday morning we were all at Mass. Johnny came to Mum and asked for a tablet. He had a headache. Mum was worried. She decided not to give him anything. Shortly after his mother arrived looking for Johnny. She said she had already given him some medication. Johnny started to vomit. Panic buttons were pushed. An ambulance was called and he was rushed to Parramatta Hospital. When I came home from Mass, Dad told me what had happened. I sat on our back steps. I had my rosary beads. I kept saying the rosary, over and over, begging God to keep our darling Johnny safe.

Johnny died a few hours later with a cerebral haemorrhage. He had had a tussle on the lounge with his brother Michael and hit his head the day before.

I remember Aunty Connie (Mum's youngest sister) came to our house screaming, "Where's Johnny?"

She was told, "He's gone Con."

"Gone, gone where?" she sobbed.

For the first and not the last time in my life, my faith was badly shaken!

My prayers had fallen on deaf ears.

I was 15 years old.

Mum had a beautiful voice. She was always singing. The neighbours would open their windows to listen to her. She never raised her voice in song again after Johnny's death.

It was just the saddest time in our lives. Death touched us all for the first time.

Mum never really recovered from the loss of Johnny. The sadness stayed with her. Every year on Johnny's birthday, Mum would bake a cake for him, with his name on it. After he died, Mum continued to do this. She and his mother then took it and left it on his grave for him. I guess she wanted to continue this little ritual.

As a teenager I thought their behaviour odd. I understand their grief now.

CHAPTER 5

TWO LITTLE ANGELS ARE BORN

I was just 17 years old when I met John. They were the days of the Wednesday and Saturday night dances at the Rivoli dance-hall at Parramatta. Parramatta was just two suburbs away from where I lived with my family at No. 1 Wallace Street, Granville, the home we had moved to when I was just two years old.

I was only allowed to go dancing if my cousin, Pattie Ryan, was accompanying me. I had to be in the door my 11pm and Mum was always waiting up for me.

Pattie lived around the corner in Railway Parade, Granville. The Ryans, Ella and Amby and their children, Pattie, Max, Michael, Robert and young Johnny who passed away when he was five years old, had always lived in my gran's house in Railway Parade, Granville. That house holds many fond memories for me. My gran died there when I was about two years old and I still remember the day she died. The story was told for many a year how the last words my gran whispered was, "All I have heard all day is that little pet's voice." As a child I was notorious for the fact that I never stopped talking.

I met John at the dance-hall and one night he asked me for the last dance. He walked me home with Pattie in tow. We started dating from there. My family were all very fond of John, particularly my older brother Jack and my mother.

John and I were married on the 21st July, 1956, just two months before I turned 20. Reflecting back I realise that neither John nor I was ready for marriage. We were completely inexperienced about life and married life, and we went into marriage knowing nothing.

I remember asking Mum to tell me what married life was about. Mum was embarrassed and she said that she knew nothing of such things.

I spent six months working on making my own wedding dress. I worked on it evenings after I came home from work. My dress was a work of art, a beautiful creation. The skirt was made of glacé nylon, like sheets of floating ice. It was heavily embroidered with fine glacé sprays of flowers. The bodice of the dress was made of glacé lace flowers and the whole dress was lined with delustered satin. I spent literally hundreds of hours on my wedding dress. On the day I was married a neighbour asked Mum, "Where ever did June get that exquisite dress?"

Mum was always so proud of me, and promptly told her I had worked on it for months.

I arrived home from work the evening before my wedding to find Mum upset, in an agitated state. Mum had decided to give my dress a final press and had burnt a hole with the iron in the front of my beautiful dress.

It was only a matter of hours before I was to be married to John at the Nuptial Mass at Holy Trinity Church, Granville, at nine o'clock the next morning. I don't recall being terribly upset. Instead I sat under a lamp into the small hours repairing the damage with more appliquéd flowers. On the big day no-one could tell the difference.

My wedding day dawned a beautiful cold July day in Sydney and everything went according to plan.

In those days girls traditionally had a "going-away outfit." My outfit was a pale blue velvet frock with a matching blue felt hat, white shoes and bag, and of course the traditional white lace gloves. I left the reception and changed from my wedding outfit into my going-away outfit. I then went back to the reception to say goodbye to the guests. The hardest thing was saying goodbye to Dad. He was crying and hugging me. I told him I was only going on a holiday and I would be back in a couple of weeks. After I came home and was back at work Dad would phone me often. He always called on the 1st of the month to say "Happy Month, Darling!"

Mum also had trouble adjusting when I married. Many a day she would catch the bus to Parramatta and have lunch with me in St John's Park.

We had planned our honeymoon at a private hotel at Forster on the North Coast of New South Wales and we both looked forward to our first aeroplane trip. It was with Butler Airlines. On our wedding night we had very little sleep. The girl in the next room moaned, groaned and cried half the night. I was so worried about her, I even wanted John to go and knock on their door, as I was sure her husband was hitting her.

I said we should call the management, but John was reluctant to interfere. The next morning at breakfast I couldn't help checking her out for bruises. She didn't have any bruises and what was more she seemed to be happy and blooming. The nightly noises continued for the remainder of our stay. It would be 15 years before I finally found out what all the moaning was about.

After we were married, John and I went to live in a garage at the back of his mother's home at Wentworthville. We had done a lot to our little home; we had even put in a kitchen. To me it was my three-room little doll's house.

About three months after we were married I visited my doctor. After talking to me and examining me he told me I was still a virgin, as there had been no penetration. Also I had to have a procedure done before I could fall pregnant. This procedure was done under anaesthetic.

My great aunt Ivy had had to have this procedure some 50 years previously.

When John brought me home I guess I was still pretty groggy, and of course my mother-in-law came down and inferred I had had an abortion. I did not know what an abortion was. God what an awful woman! I talked it over with Mum. Mum knew something finally; she knew what an abortion was.

When I think about it now, it was just so sad really. Here I was, married with all these awful things happening to me and really, I should have been home safe and secure in my own bedroom, with my family. I was still an immature young girl, too young for marriage. I had been plunged into all of this after 19 years of being overprotected. This should never have been allowed to happen.

I sincerely believe it was only through the 'grace of God' that I fell pregnant with my first child immediately after that procedure, but as my stomach grew,

I bloomed. I was over the moon.

My pregnancy was a wonderful time. I was happier than I had ever been. "It will be twin boys I am sure," I said.

"Heaven forbid," replied my mum. She obviously lived more in the real world than I did. By the time I was three months pregnant I was in maternity clothes and I wanted the world to know about it. "Little Junee Ollerenshaw is pregnant!" I sang to the world.

Well I didn't get my twin boys. Instead I gave birth to my wonderful and perfect little Cathy on 11th June, 1957, six weeks premature and weighing in at just less than six pounds. Cathy was a beautiful baby and John was beaming. Cathy would become the light of his life. There would never be another child born to compare to her.

Due to my earlier gynaecological problems I was told I

would never carry a child full term, but this was better than not being able to carry one at all.

My mother in law said "The neighbours will have the clock on you, wearing maternity clothes and nothing there to hide." But that didn't bother me. I didn't care; I wanted the world to know.

A short time before Cathy was born I still only had a small bump on my tummy. One night John came home from work and told me he had been telling the guys at work how enormous I was, and they said he should help me in and out of the bath as I could get awkward and fall. I guess I looked enormous to him.

When Cathy was born there was great carry-on about her name. Being a modern miss I thought I would call her Zoe, but this met with opposition from both John's and my families. When I suggested Jenny, the mother-in-law, who didn't impress me at the best of times, started dancing around singing, "She's a Jenny, and she's a Jenny, a little Jenny wren." That was the finish of the name Jenny for me, so Cathy was settled on and a little Cathy she was. Her name really suited her. She was a real little Cathy.

When Cathy was born even the nurses in the hospital said, "She is the image of her father." She had long, black, curly hair and beautiful, clear olive skin. I can still see ma-in-law Minnie dancing around saying "She's one of us, she's one of us. We can't blame the milkman for this one."

We were horrified. "What an awful old woman," mumbled my darling mum.

However, when she came along, my second daughter, Lyndy, was more like my side of the family. And yet despite this, the girls always bore a strong resemblance to each other.

Although both girls were born with curly, black hair, they both went blonde very quickly.

My Aunty Kit, who worked in a lingerie factory, made Cathy a wardrobe fit for a princess. She made three complete outfits, pink, blue and white, bonnets, dresses and petticoats. I guess everyone was just so happy for me. And although Mum and I always were a bit suspicious about where all this beautiful fabric and lace came from, we kept it to ourselves. Aunty Kit said, "Oh, just off-cuts, don't worry, just off-cuts." But we still wondered!

I would dress my darling Cathy in her beautiful outfits on a Saturday morning, put her in the pram and Dad would take her out shopping. She was like a little Dresden doll. Dad would invariably come home to us and say, "I couldn't get a thing done; every bugger stopped me to look at her. Do you realise she'll be Miss Australia in 20 years."

Unfortunately, Lyndy was to be my last child. I would have loved those five children. However, this was not meant to be.

If Cathy was my self-sufficient child, Lyndy was my clinging vine, my shadow and my Mum's little darling. Mum had five granddaughters in her lifetime and three more and two grandsons were born after her death.

However, Lyndy was her little sweetheart and she adored her.

All of her life Cathy had an overactive mind and an overactive body. She was a true little Gemini child. She had a unique alertness about her and actually learnt to talk before she learnt to walk. When we were living with Mum and Dad before Lyndy was born, she would stand up and hold on to her cot. I can still see her calling "Toast, toast," to my dad in the early morning as soon as she heard him in the kitchen.

Mum and Dad thought she was so smart, and of course she would always get her morning toast.

Whenever I put Cathy in her cot to sleep day or night I always patted her off to sleep. At times it took my breath away when I looked at this perfectly formed tiny bundle. I had created her, she was a part of me, and I had created her!

The gentlest, most contented and rewarding time of my life was when the girls were babies. That was my time. John was so good to me in those days. He would come home from work some nights and the dishes would still be in the sink, but he would hop in and help with the dinner, and all the other chores. I would have spent much of my day playing with and just caring for the girls.

When the girls were around three and four years old, one morning there was a knock at the front door. Smiling, I opened the door. I soon had the smile wiped off my face. This red-faced woman was shaking her finger at me. In broken English she shouted, "You have the rudest children. They are harassing me and doing bad things!"

"Out! Out! Off with you, my children are perfect!" I insisted.

The girls were too young to question about this, so I thought I would watch and see what was happening. A couple of days later I stood at the lounge-room window watching. There was a bus stop outside our house.

There they were hiding behind the trellis, peeping out, poking their tongues out in unison at this red-faced, furious woman. Then they would duck back behind the trellis and double up with laughter. I thought it was just the funniest scene.

I had never seen them poke their tongues out before. This would be a good story for Mum and I to have a laugh about I thought.

I opened the window and called out, "Come on, girls, come and have a drink." They came in straight-faced looking at each other as if to say, "She thinks we're perfect. But we know different don't we?"

All through their lives they had this secret, sharing closeness.

I realised it was not always a good idea to ask Lyndy to keep a secret. One year her father's birthday was coming up and I had bought two flannelette shirts for him. I said to her, "Now, Lyndy, not a word to Daddy about the shirts." I can still see her shaking her darling little blonde head, rolling her eyes and saying, "Now, Daddy, you can't have two shirts for your birthday. Mummy hasn't got two shirts for you for your birthday." Then she turned to me still shaking her head "You haven't, have you, Mummy?" We all just laughed.

I was preparing breakfast one Sunday morning when I heard Cathy screaming. I ran to see what was happening. She was lying on the floor in the hall, blood pouring from a cut above her right eye. Then Lyndy appeared, and she had a cut in exactly the same position above her left eye and blood streaming down her face. Neither John nor I waited to inquire what had happened. We rushed them both to Fairfield Hospital.

It seems the girls had been playing in the garden and they had had a fight. Cathy hit Lyndy with a brick. She panicked when she saw the blood, and was running to tell me, when she fell and hit her own head on the edge of the bookcase. Mum soon arrived at the hospital with John.

Mum's main worry was, "What will people think? Everyone will assume they have been fighting." That statement broke the tension for me and I started to laugh. What did it matter if these two little ones had had a fight? There was not a lot of harm done. The girls carried their identical scars all of their lives.

Around this same time, I was having a sleep-in one Sunday morning. I was lying there thinking "The house seems unusually quiet, I had better get up see what's going on."

Lyndy was seated on the commode with a tea towel tied around her neck. Cathy was standing behind her. She had a tea towel tied around her hair, and she had my scissors in her hand. Lyndy's hair had been cut to about one inch long on one side and dangling down to her shoulders on the other side.

Mum and Dad had this ongoing argument about Lyndy's hair. Dad always believed children's hair should be cut short. He always said, "Long hair takes all your strength." However,

Mum was determined Lyndy's hair would stay long like Cathy's. The problem was Cathy had wonderful thick hair, whereas Lyndy's hair was thin and straggly. Mum spent a fortune on Lyndy's hair. She tried everything on the market, expensive shampoos and oils but nothing seemed to improve the thickness or texture.

When I surveyed this scene my first thought was "What will Mum say?" "Cathy, whatever are you doing?" I asked.

Cathy did her thing; struck her usual pose, hands on hips, nose in the air. "I agree with Poppy!" she said. "A good haircut is what she needs!"

It seemed I had a very self-opinionated, precocious, four-year-old child on my hands.

The local hairdresser was our first stopping point the next morning. Then we were off to catch the train and bus to see Nanny and face the music. Lyndy actually looked good with her new pixie hairstyle, I thought.

Finally we arrived at Nanny's. Mum was almost in tears and totally devastated.

But the haircut was the best thing to happen to Lyndy. Forever after her hair grew thick and lustrous; she ended up with lovely long, thick plaits.

The next time Lyndy had her haircut was many years later and for a completely different reason. However, Cathy was involved again.

I went to collect Lyndy from Mum's place one afternoon. Mum was sound asleep in her favourite chair with Lyndy perched beside her on the arm of the chair. When I walked through the door she put her tiny finger on her lips for me to be quiet and not wake Nanny, while she proceeded with sticking bandaids all over Mum's face and arms, I thought it was just the funniest sight and hoped Mum wouldn't be needing a bandaid tonight. Lyndy did not laugh, she was deadly serious about the whole thing. I went into the bathroom and here in Mum's snow-white bath, the pride of her life, the bath that was never to have a spot on it, was a broken bottle of triple dye. Oh dear God, Lyndy had certainly kept herself amused; she had had a wonderful day. I was trying to clean the bath when I heard Mum say, "She's a shocking child." I turned around and there was Mum, still covered in bandaids! I burst out laughing.

I thought later I might have been better crying, as Mum just became more upset at me laughing at her. It was something we laughed about later though.

Cathy 5 years old, Lyndy 4 years old, with Santa at Grace Bros.

Cathy and Lyndy off to visit Nan.

Cathy and Lyndy sharing a secret and a giggle.

CHAPTER 6

PRIVILEDGED CHILDHOODS

When the girls were still very young I applied for a job with the local driving school teaching driving. Old Mac who owned the driving school gave me some instructions and then he employed me. I was to be teaching in one of his cars, a Volkswagen Beetle. I became the first female driving instructor to haunt the streets of Sydney. Fortunately, licensing of instructors did not come in for a few years, as I had not been driving all that long when I started teaching .The job was great as I could work my hours around dropping the girls off to Mum before work and collecting them after work. I worked for Mac for a year or so, then I went to a larger school where I made a lot of friends. This job opened up a whole new world to me. I stayed with L. & D. for a number of years. Eventually I became tired of working for bosses, and I decided I would start my own business. Yes, it was time to start my own driving school I decided.

This was to be my first business venture. I called my business Patience Driving School. And I soon had more work than I really needed.

I found a lot of women preferred a woman teacher. And lots of men preferred their wife to be taught by another woman. I often wondered if PDS was such a good idea for a name, as I would sometimes have a book full of difficult pupils. In those days, fortunately, I had nerves of steel, the patience of a saint. I was 30 years old and they were good years for me, probably my best, happiest, most carefree years really. I was no longer the molly-coddled girl I had been before I had children. I now had to support us, put the food on the table. I was out there, exposed to the world for the first time really. A time of wine, friends and song I guess. I was earning good money and had lovely friends. The girls were going to Our Lady Of Mercy, a Catholic girl's college at Parramatta, and both of them were happy at school.

The driving-school crowd were a decent lot in those days. There was an affinity between the instructors and inspectors.

In the early days, we had a lot of fun, and we were all out to help each other, most of the time. We worked together and socialised together. On Sundays we would pile children, food and picnic gear into our respective cars and head for the beach. Wattamolla was a favourite beach for us all, and of course one of the guys, Noel, a Police Testing Officer always brought a keg of beer in his utility. I always tied red ribbons in the girls' hair, so I could see them easily as they frolicked in the water.

One day Cathy went missing, and I was frantic. A search was quickly set up for her. However, it was over an hour before she was found. She was sitting in a caravan with an elderly couple having a cup of tea. I had imagined her drowned in the sea by that time and I was sobbing my heart out. Cathy was completely unperturbed

Before I started my own business I was working for a guy who had a flying licence and once a month he, two other instructors and myself would all throw in our share for the hire of a light plane. We usually went up in a four-seater Victa out of Bankstown airport. At that time my dearest wish was to have some flying lessons. I knew I would never be able to afford to acquire a licence; just some lessons would have been great.

About this time I won some money in the NSW State lottery and I thought to myself, "I'm going to keep quiet about this or it will be eaten up with household bills."

I had had a few lessons and one day I was booked in for a lesson and something went wrong. Mum could not mind the girls, so I phoned to cancel my lesson. My instructor's wife answered the phone and said, "Oh, that's okay, June, you can leave the girls with me, it's only an hour, I can keep them amused for that time."

"Oh gee that's great, thank you," I said. Now that was a big mistake. I had my lesson and was feeling elated and on the way home I said to Lyndy "Now, Lyndy, not a word to Nanny about this."

I really enjoyed my flying lessons. I was so enthralled. I learnt you had to keep the wheel parallel with the horizon. I don't remember learning much else. I felt good about myself when I could tell my friends I was having flying lessons.

A couple of days later we were at Nan's place and Lyndy said, "Nanny, Mummy didn't go up, up, up in the big aeroplane, no Nanny, Cathy and I did not stay with the lady while she went up in the aeroplane. No Nanny, Mummy would never do that. Would you, Mummy!"

My mum was furious with me. By the time Mum finished telling me how irresponsible I was I had decided not to have any more lessons, and anyway the money had just about run out. However, I did not forsake my monthly flights with the boys. But I always made sure Lyndy knew nothing of this.

After our flights we usually went to the local hotel for a beer and a meal.

A couple of years later my instructor crashed his Victa and lost his life. Fortunately he was flying alone.

My life was surely running a different course these days. These excursions certainly helped me to tolerate the abuse at home. It was something I had never been able to discuss with anyone.

Cathy makes her First Communion.

Lyndy making her debut, meeting the Bishop.

CHAPTER 7

LIFE WITH JOHN

After Cathy was born John and I moved in with Mum and Dad. It was fast approaching Christmas 1958. We had been living with Mum and Dad for about a year. Cathy was 18 months old, Lyndy a baby of three months. Finally, we had saved a deposit for our own home.

After looking at a lovely, new Jennings home, we finally decided on an older home in Day Street, Lansvale, just around the corner from Tom Ugley's nightclub on the Hume Highway. John felt sure we could renovate and make it liveable. It didn't have a stove and the loo was down the back garden, but I was not at all daunted.

First, we set about fumigating. Mum was a great help with fumigating, cleaning away cobwebs and dumping rubbish. John and I set off to Toongabbie on the train, to the second-hand shop. We arrived home with grandfather chairs, a coffee table and odds and ends, all on the train with us. John had a mate with a utility bring the blue Early Kooka stove home for us. It was a very old stove, but I thought it was wonderful. I was happy to have a stove all of my own. Then John set about making a double bed and a built-in lounge.

Even though some of our friends had new homes, I can never remember envying them. The house cost £5,000. The old lady who owned it carried the finance for us at 5% reducible interest. The repayments were £5 per week. The new Jennings house was 6% flat interest, so we believed we had done the right thing.

However, in retrospect, the task John had set himself may have helped escalate his mental-health problems and ultimately contributed to the breakdown of our marriage.

John worked on the railways as a carriage builder and he was confident about the task he had set himself. But, over the next couple of years a radical change took place in him.

Perhaps the problems were always there and I had just not seen them. Just the same the renovations exerted a lot of pressure on him. He became more and more stressed, and began to walk around the house talking and laughing to himself.

As the months rolled on and the renovations continued, John became more and more unstable. There was many a Saturday John would be acting strange and decide to go to the hotel. I'd pack a bag, put the girls in the car and drive to Mum's place to stay for a couple of days. When we came home he never inquired where we had been. The girls probably told him we had been to Nan's and he was always glad to have us back again. I would drive all around the back streets rather than have to pass the hotel where he drank. I was always so afraid of him.

Looking back I wonder why we never really communicated. We never discussed the problems in our marriage. I guess communication comes with maturity, something neither of us had at that time.

When the girls were approximately 3 and 4 he started to be abusive and threatening to me. On top of that, he stopped financially supporting us. Lyndy was staying with Mum for a few days as she often did and one day after a drinking bout we had words. John grabbed Cathy and the car keys. He ran out with her and jumped into the car. I was panic-stricken! I did not wait to lock the front door or take off my apron. I never knew what to expect when he had been drinking. I grabbed Cathy from him and held her in my arms as I jumped into the passenger seat of the car just as he was taking off.

We were travelling over Silverwater Bridge at about 60 miles per hour, I held Cathy tightly in my arms. Neither Cathy nor I uttered a sound.

Suddenly he pulled into a service station and got out of the car. I immediately slid over behind the wheel. I sat there terrified; I was shaking violently not knowing what to expect next as I just sat there waiting for him. He soon came back and jumped into the passenger seat. He was calm again. He said, "You're lucky I needed to go to the toilet. I was going to kill the three of us."

Everything came to a head just after Christmas 1964. John had been drinking heavily over that Christmas period.

At this stage, even though I saw Mum most days, I had not said much about what had been going on. She was always so sick with her heart problems, I tried not to worry her. One Saturday John was acting strangely. He had been drinking, he was talking and laughing to himself. He got in the car and drove off. Unbeknown to me, he went to Mum's house and insisted on bringing her over to our home, even though she was extremely ill that day. She, of course, came home with him. She felt something was drastically wrong. Mum later informed me she had been aware of his erratic behaviour for some time. I had never discussed my life in Day Street, Lansvale with anyone, not even Mum.

Mum had given Cathy a scooter and Lyndy a three-wheeler bike for Christmas, via Santa Claus. During the course of the afternoon Lyndy was riding her bike around the lounge room.

"Look, Nanny, look how good I am!" she shouted excitedly.

I'm not sure what happened next, however, John smacked Lyndy on the leg, probably not hard, but too hard for Mum. Like me, Mum did not believe in smacking children. An awful argument broke out. I took the girls and headed for the back garden. "I'll leave them to it," I thought. But, things just deteriorated as the day went on. John ordered Mum out of the house.

"I'm not going anywhere!" she said adamantly.

Then he started giggling to himself, pacing up and down, up and down, click, click, click, click on the polished floors. How often I had listened to that sound for hours on end during the night. Click, click, click, click.

Somehow we got through the day, had our dinner, put the girls to bed, then Mum and I went to bed. Mum was a worried mother and grandmother. I fell into an exhausted sleep and slept soundly all night. Not so poor old Mum.

"I sat up in bed all night long. I have never experienced a night like that before," she told me the next day. John had paced up and down, up and down, all night long. "He had a carving knife in his hand," she informed me gravely.

The next morning, as usual, it was as if nothing strange had occurred the day or night before. John went off to work. Mum and I sat and talked. And talk we did for hours. I told everything that had been happening to me in my life with John. She was shocked.

The thing I remember most of what was said that morning was Mum saying, "My pet, I was sure we would all die in our beds."

I told her how he would sit me on a stool in front of the dressing-table mirror, maybe for an hour, even more sometimes. I had to look in the mirror and "confess"; "You are a stupid, narrow-minded bitch, you are a stupid, narrow-minded bitch." This seemed to always happen when he had been drinking. His behaviour always followed a pattern of stress, alcohol, moods, pacing up and down and sitting me in front of the mirror.

One night he picked me up and threw me over the back of the lounge (all six stone of me). I was unhurt, but terrified. Strangely enough there were rarely ever any arguments. I always thought of it as one of his spells. At this time John was riding a motorbike to work. I often remember praying he would be killed on the road coming home from work, asking God to just not let him walk through the door again.

I just didn't know how we could continue this nightmare of an existence. I seem to have obliterated from my memory many of the awful things he did and said. However, I can never erase the thought of my praying to God for him to die on the road. It now seems such an appalling thing to pray for.

John would often sit on the side of my bed and hold the sheet hard against my throat, and giggle while I cried. Forty-five years later, I still, occasionally, wake in the night, pushing the sheet away from my throat.

I packed some clothes that day, and the girls and I all went home to live with Mum and Dad for the time being. "It's certainly not safe for you or the girls there," Mum observed.

We were not sure what was going to happen next. But, through all of this, neither Mum nor I judged John. We both knew something was radically wrong. Mum had always thought the world of him. He was a wonderful son-in-law to her.

A few days later in the very early morning there was a knock on the door. I answered it and John was standing there. He was unshaven, unkempt, and neglected-looking. Poor John had been through a bad few days so it seemed and he had come to me for help.

Yes, the black mood had passed. He was this lovely person again. I felt safe again. But, I was in for a long day. We sat in Mum's lounge-room holding hands and talking for several hours. Later I went with John to the local GP. The doctor had written a letter and advised me to go with him to Parramatta Psychiatric Hospital.

John decided he wanted to go home to collect some things. I drove him out to our home at Lansvale. He fiddled around for hours. Would he go to hospital? Would he not go to hospital? I made no ripples, as always, just stayed with it. It was late afternoon before we arrived at the hospital. John talked to two different psychiatrists. This went on all afternoon and into the evening.

Eventually, a magistrate was called in. John was certified insane. He was diagnosed with paranoid schizophrenia. His family was in shock. My kin was in shock. Everyone blamed me. It was New Years Eve. That day left its mark on my heart. I have never to this day found New Years Eve to be a happy time.

John was in hospital for many months during which time he had a series of electric-shock treatments. The shock treatment blocked out all the bad things that had been going on. But I felt it had taken away his spark, his "alive-ness". The whole time he was in the hospital Mum and I took turns in visiting him. He really looked forward to his packet of Rothmans cigarettes. We gave him a day's rations at a time, otherwise they would be stolen or given away.

One day, he demanded, "June, if you don't bring the girls in tomorrow to see me, I'll come out! Just walk out. I need to see the girls!" I wasn't sure if he could walk out, but then I had often seen the other inmates walking the streets of Parramatta, and although I hated the thought of taking Cathy and Lyndy into that place, I took them the next day. Sure enough, he had forgotten all about wanting to see them by then. He was vague and obviously under heavy sedation.

I was in a strange new world when I visited him in the psychiatric hospital, surrounded by men and women, some of whom, no, many of whom, told me they were Napoleon, Henry VIII or Cleopatra. We even had Jesus Christ in our midst. Mostly, they believed themselves to be famous people from history. They never seemed to change their personage. I was sitting with him one morning when another inmate came in. She leant over and whispered in his ear.

He patted her on the arm and said as he smiled at her, "Yes, Elaine, later." She walked off with a deadpan look on her face.

I said to him, "What was that all about?"

"Oh, she wants me to have sex with her. She will forget about it for a while now. She is in for stabbing her husband because he would not have sex with her."

Oh God, I thought, *what next?* She certainly knows how to pick her men! When I arrived home from work one night, Elaine was sitting on the front fence waiting for me, wielding a nail file. I was panic-stricken. I locked myself in the car, put my hand on the horn and kept it there until Mum and Dad came out to me.

She then left. I never did find out how she got our address. Some of the patients seemed to come and go as they pleased from the hospital.

One night, I went in to see John and he had been restrained, strapped down to his bed. I can't explain what he looked like. It was just awful. This whole scene terrified me. I eventually found a nurse and asked her what had happened to him.

The nurse nonchantly replied, "Oh, don't worry, he'll be okay. He has lockjaw." One of the other patients had got out, gone to the pub and brought back a bottle of vodka. "Straight vodka doesn't mix too well with the drugs," remarked the nurse, as she walked away. I ran outside and brought up my dinner. That was not the last time I would lose a meal in the same way after visiting that place. It was life as I never imagined it could be. The place horrified me! I had led a very sheltered life and now I was thrown into this. But, somehow, I just hung in there.

One day I ran into one of John's siblings in the street. There were harsh words about what I had done to her brother.

All I could say was, "If you care so much, you should try living with him." Unless you have lived with a paranoid schizophrenic person, you could never know what it is like. The highs. The lows. You never know how it is going to be from one day to the next.

Around this time, I was told John's father had committed suicide when John was a young boy. His father had hung himself and it was John who had found him. I don't remember exactly how long John was in the psychiatric hospital, just that it was a long time. I spent many hours there. The inmates all seemed to walk with a robotic stiffness. I thought it must have been the drugs they were taking or perhaps the shock treatment. Today, I can pick people with this illness a distance away and I still feel sad.

I had been working as a driving instructor for 14 years and at this time I was teaching a young girl whom I had got to know quite well. One day while she was having her lesson with me, she said rather calmly, "My dad died yesterday." I was shocked and said how sorry I was.

"Oh, don't be!" she replied, "I'm not. I'm glad." Then she proceeded to tell me about her relationship with her father and how he had sexually interfered with her.

Somehow I got through the lesson with her. I then drove to Parramatta Park. This was a place to which I often went when I had some serious thinking to do. I sat in the park, looking at the trees, listening to the birds singing. I had never heard of incest and did not know such a thing existed. Somehow I suddenly felt uneasy, and a terrible fear overtook me. There were a lot of big decisions I had to make about my life and the future of my girls, and I had a lot of things to think through regarding John and my marriage.

The next morning I made an appointment with John's psychiatrist to discuss the grave concerns I had about living with him after he was discharged.

His words to me were, "June, he related a lot of

confidentialities to me about his personal relationship with his older daughter, during the period of his shock treatment. However, it's my sole purpose to protect my patient. It is, therefore, my aim to get you and your daughters back together with your husband."

I knew I could never expose Cathy to living with her father again.

By the end of the day I had grown up a lot. School was in. I was now a pupil in the school of hard knocks. Believe you me, that was just the beginning, and what a beginning it was!

I had a decision to make, but really there was no deciding, no option for me. I had two darling little daughters to protect, rear and educate. My marriage was over. Six years after marrying John I set fire to my beautiful wedding dress in the back garden along with my wedding and engagement rings. My mum stood there crying. I didn't shed a tear. My tears had long since dried up.

My Aunt Ella came with me to pack up our things. We came across several knives that I had obviously hidden away over the years. They were tucked into drawers and cupboards, hidden from harm's way, all wrapped in tea towels or towels. We obviously had had some lucky breaks. Still today, over 45 years later, I do not have a carving knife in my home.

Between going to see John, looking after Mum, whose health was deteriorating, taking the girls to school and continuing to work to support us, life was really full-on.

On top of all my other problems, Lyndy, my emotionally fragile child, had decided she was not going to go to school. I always saw Lyndy as fragile. She was often sick as a toddler. Mum forever had her at the doctor. She did not adapt to changing schools as easily as Cathy did. So there I was every morning, trudging up the steps with Lyndy, her little arms and legs locked around me. She would be begging me not to make her go to school. Sister Mary would come out and take her from me. She was very patient with her, but I would retreat down the stairs, always crying, sobbing quietly morning after morning. I was thankful Cathy had such a placid and easygoing nature. She loved school, the nuns and the Catholic Church's teachings.

By now Mum was really frail and her health was failing rapidly. It was early morning on 5th May and I had been up most of the night with her because she was having trouble breathing, but she did not want to go back to hospital. "Come on, darling," I pleaded. "I promise I won't leave you there, I just want to get some oxygen for you, and then I'll bring you back home again."

Why I did not call an ambulance I can now only wonder. I half dragged and half carried Mum out to my car. When we arrived at the hospital I can still remember this little nun coming out to me and saying, "It's best if she is taken, my dear, she is suffering a lot."

I was stunned. "This cannot be" I thought, "not Mum, nothing is going to happen to my precious mother." Mum had always been there for me and I felt I could not exist without her. I then whispered to myself aloud, "Stupid old woman, she doesn't know what she's talking about, Mum's not going to die."

The next day she was still in hospital and I had been with her all day. It was getting on in the afternoon. Mum was straining to see the clock,

"Don't worry, darling!" I said, "I'm going to pick up the girls from school now. I'll give them something to eat and we'll be back in to see you soon."

I was just about to set the meal on the table when my cousin Robert came. "Come quickly," he urged, "your mother has had a bad turn, she is very ill."

When we arrived back at the hospital there was a nun at the door waiting for us. "Your mother has just passed away," she told me.

It was precisely 6pm on the 6th of May, 1966.

I remember running through the hospital, screaming hysterically. When I got to Mum's bed, I picked her up in my arms and hugged her. Her body was warm. I started to scream again. "She can't be dead, she's still warm." The little nun came and spoke to me, and then she gave me a dose of green medicine. Whatever the medicine was, I became almost instantly in control. She made me a hot cup of tea and I got myself together and set about informing our relatives and friends of Mum's death.

Mum had finally given in after a 50 year struggle with heart problems. The illness she had lived with since she was seven years old had finally beaten her.

I sat out on the back patio the whole night long, all alone. May in Sydney is a cold month, but I don't remember feeling cold. Here I was 30 years of age and I knew nothing of death. I had always assumed that when you died you would go cold immediately. I had never really had an occasion to think about death to this extent. My parents had overprotected me in the extreme. To my own detriment!

When morning came I was more convinced than ever that Mum was not dead.

She had still been warm to my touch the night before. During the morning a friend of mine called around to our place and I said to him, "I have to go to the hospital to see Mum, but I don't think I should drive." He readily agreed to drive me to see my mum.

When we arrived the little nun was in her office. I knocked on her door ,"I've come to see my mum." I said.

The nun took me into the back garden of the hospital to see Mum. She was in a lovely little room in this beautiful garden. I picked her up in my arms and kissed her beloved face, the face I loved so dearly. I was shocked. She was cold. The expression on her face told me only one thing. "I don't want to go. I don't want to leave you and my darling Cathy and Lyndy."

Shock and grief had set in; it was like nothing I had ever

experienced. I dressed completely in black for months. I even wore a black ribbon around my head to bed. There was no-one there to help me. I tried several times to talk to Dad, but he always broke down in tears and walked away. They had been married for 35 years and never really been separated. Grief counselling was unheard of in those days and my parents had overprotected me to the extreme. I had never been exposed to death. They really had not done me any favours.

I could not bring myself to tell the girls that their beloved Nanny had died until one day my brother Jack threatened to tell them if I didn't. I promised him I would tell them soon. Somehow I just didn't get around to it.

Some months later Cathy made her confirmation, and afterwards when we were standing outside the church someone I knew came up to me and said, "June, I'm so sorry to hear you lost your mother."

I just froze! Cathy and Lyndy were standing there with me.

The girls had never asked me where Nanny was or when she was coming home from hospital.

On the way home, Cathy said to me, "Mummy, Lyndy and I have talked about this. We thought Nanny had died and you were too upset to talk about it to us. We love you, we will look after you, always." I was stunned and ashamed. Really, these two little girls were being far more mature than I was. I made a conscious decision that day that I would take the girls to any funeral that may come up in the future. And I did. I had decided they were going to experience life, and be exposed to it, as I had never been.

CHAPTER 8

HOLIDAYS ON THE GOLD COAST

The girls and I travelled to the Gold Coast every May and August in the school holidays. They were wonderful years for us. I usually tried to stay at a different motel each time we came. We played I spy and sang Peter, Paul and Mary songs all along the coast highway every year.

I would pack everything in the car. Lyndy always said, "Mum always takes everything but the kitchen sink, and she would take that if I didn't watch her." We were all packed to go home one time and I couldn't find the car keys. I had locked them in the boot with the kitchen sink. Oh dear, what a business. I had to pull the back seat out and everything else to find the keys. Lyndy was as tactless as ever and was talking about me taking fry pans, etc. She made sure to tell everyone all about it when we arrived home.

One year we were preparing for our epic drive to Queensland when Cathy contracted tonsillitis. We took her to the family doctor. Dr Boyde said she would be able to travel in a few days, however, it was best if we travelled by train and we must have a sleeper compartment. After ringing the railway to inquire about a sleeper, I was informed they were fully booked. Everyone was in tears. So I phoned the doctor. "June, go to the booking office in an hour and there will be a sleeper cabin ticket for you." Yes, he had pulled some strings. We got our sleeping compartment, however, there was only one bed, a double bunk. I said, "Lyndy, you're on the top bunk and you're to stay there. No drinks of water, no toilet emergencies, just go up there and sleep. I will sleep in the bottom bunk with Cathy." I was deeply concerned about her. Lyndy did as she was told for once. One big problem was that Lyndy had two thick plaits that fell to her waist. She was not allowed to go up and down the ladder. However, these plaits had the habit of falling in my face many times during the night. She spent the whole night either telling me something or checking up on Cathy. Dangling by her toes with her plaits in my face, I was glad to see the end of the train journey.

We ate takeaway meals and were among the first Aussies to sample Kentucky Fried Chicken. Sitting on the beach, eating our meal out of a box, was unheard of. We became aware that people nearby were staring at us. This was so new. Colonel Sanders had arrived in Australia. We all got the giggles. That was the era of picnic baskets and food from home. "Oh well," chirped Lyndy, "at least we are up with the times. Something else to tell Angie about when we get home."

Oh how the girls loved to swim. It may have been winter down south, not so in Queensland. Life on the Gold Coast was very casual in the 1960s. We wandered around in our bikinis and bare feet. I was so carefree nothing fazes me. They would swim until they started to shiver, then they would run inside and have a hot shower and then back into the pool. The hot showers ran all day and we ended up with very wet carpets. I always had to bring heaps of spare towels with me. I felt we would not have been the best of tenants.

In May 1967 I decided it was a good time to take Dad away

for a break as it was coming up to the first anniversary of Mum's death.

From the moment Lyndy could tell the time she was forever asking, "Poppy, what time is it right now?" At night she would wake up and go into his room, tap him on the shoulder and say to him again, "Poppy what time is it?" He was so patient with her, but he finally bought the girls a watch each. I still have those little watches in my drawer.

On 6th May we were sitting waiting for our meal in a restaurant in Surfers Paradise. Dad and I were sitting there and both feeling sad – talking about anything but Mum's anniversary. Suddenly Lyndy said, "Poppy, what time is it right now?" It was right on six. Dad burst into tears and left the table. I gently explained to the girls that it was exactly one year since Nanny's death.

Lyndy, Me and Cathy on Surfer's Paradise Beach.

CHAPTER 9

MY MIRACLE CHILD

When Cathy was 10 years old she had been having a lot of headaches and I had taken her to the local general practitioner, Dr Boyde, a number of times.

"Oh, June, you worry too much. She's probably going to be a migraine sufferer like you, and your mother before you," he remarked nonchalantly.

One morning very early, I awoke to the sound of Cathy vomiting. "Darling, what has made you sick?" I asked worriedly. It was then she then told me that she had been vomiting in the early mornings for some time.

"Mummy, I'll be okay. I did not want to worry you!" she answered.

I felt a panic feeling in the pit of my stomach. My motherly instinct told me there was something seriously wrong with Cathy, so I took her back to the doctor. He still felt there was no reason for my concern.

"She is okay," he reinforced me.

I was still unsatisfied with this and decided to take Cathy

to the children's hospital in Camperdown in the city of Sydney for their diagnosis that very morning. We saw an intern, Dr Brian Carney. He did not treat this ailment flippantly. Cathy was given tests and X-rays immediately.

Later in the day, he told me he would have to admit her to hospital immediately with a suspected brain tumour. I was to be told later, that early morning vomiting was one of the symptoms of a brain tumour.

Cathy took the whole thing very calmly, but Lyndy and I were both devastated by Cathy's illness.

Dr Carney was correct. Cathy had a tumour on her brain and she was to spend many months in hospital. I kept repeating to myself, she definitely has a brain tumour. Cathy definitely has a tumour on her brain.

Forty odd years on I can still remember. It was called an astrocytoma situated in the hypothalamus.

When I was told Cathy had to face brain surgery, I was devastated. Then they told me they would have to shave off her beautiful, waist-length blonde hair. For me that was just the worst thing. I had never seen either of my girls without hair.

We decided not to tell her until the morning of the operation that her hair was to be shaved off, not until after she had been sedated. I remember the ward sister was crying. She took off her cap to show me her own long, black, waist-length hair as she said tearfully, "I could not bear to lose my crowning glory."

After the operation I looked at her and thought, "This is the first time I have seen my darling Cathy without hair and she is even more beautiful than ever." I was amazed how angelic she looked.

On the morning of the day she was to have the operation, I arrived at the hospital very early. There were nurses and doctors around her bed. I immediately knew something was radically wrong. They had fans blowing on her and she was wrapped in wet sheets.

The medical staff informed me that Cathy was a very sick little girl. She had a raging temperature.

With a grave face the doctor informed me, "We have to operate as soon as her temperature comes down. The fluid is building up in her brain from the tumour. The pressure has to be relieved."

Cathy underwent an arduous operation. They had warned me she could die on the operating table. I stood there unable to speak; unable to believe I could lose my darling little 10-year-old child.

In times of trauma our reasoning takes on a completely new pattern of thinking. I remember sitting on a stool outside the operating room all alone praying for her. Asking God to spare her. I sat there for five hours and 10 minutes. I had convinced myself if I sat facing the door she would survive. I recalled previously sitting on this same stool while she had had, compared to this, relatively minor surgery. Also, waiting anxiously in the passageway that day were parents of a baby boy, one of their twins. Those parents had sat with their backs to the door and their baby had not survived and I had experienced the doctor coming to tell them their sad news. Hence, I felt I was not to turn my back on that door. I was certain if I sat facing it, Cathy would pull through.

With prayer and positive thinking she survived the operation. However, they were not able to remove the tumour. She would have it for ever. As the tumour was entwined in the nerve centre of her brain it was too dangerous to tamper with so the doctor told me.

They did a biopsy and it was malignant, a rapidly growing growth, and they told me they would start chemotherapy as soon as she recovered from the operation.

I always thought of myself as a compassionate person and yet there were children in that ward dying all around me, but I felt nothing for them.

I guess I was so overcome with what was happening to

my beautiful little girl that I had nothing left for these other children. I still remember looking at all these little ones and feeling quite detached from their problems.

Every morning I would arrive at the hospital early enough to give Cathy her bath and fresh nightie.

One morning I arrived and she was very distressed because a little girl in her ward had died in the night. I calmed her down and read a story to her, and it was then that I became aware that I felt no sadness for the child who had died. I was just glad that Cathy was still hanging in there.

Her bed was not empty. She was still alive

A short time after Cathy had been in hospital, I came home one evening and there on my bed was the most beautiful little dressing gown I had ever seen. It was Cathy's favourite colour; teal blue, with white checks, quilted, and the yoke was a mass of lace.

I burst into tears and sat on the bed holding it to my heart and Lyndy came and put her arms around me. She had a beautiful smile on her face. She had gone to our "tin" and taken the money we were saving for Lyndy's own birthday. She then went to David Jones store at Parramatta, just two minutes walk away from our home in Victoria Road, and told them she wanted the best dressing gown they had in the store for her sister who was very ill in hospital. Cathy loved that gown.

Lyndy was all of nine years of age.

I drove from Parramatta to the hospital every morning of Cathy's many stays in hospital. One morning when I arrived Cathy was not in her bed. On inquiring from the nurse where she was, I was told, "Oh, Cathy is in the reception room," she said. Princess Alexandra was coming to the hospital that morning and some of the children had been taken to meet her.

I was not impressed! She was so ill at this time. Shaking with temper I marched out of the ward and over to the reception room, I picked her up and carried her back to bed.

"Oh Mummy, I'm so glad you've come. I have a terrible headache," she cried.

I went to the ward sister to ask for a painkiller for her.

"Oh, she will have to wait. Nurse will be taking the medications around in half an hour," she said.

I saw red! I picked up something from her desk and said angrily, "If you don't give me something immediately, I will smash that glass cabinet and get it for myself!" She apologised and quickly gave me some painkillers for Cathy. The nursing in the Children's Hospital was really very good in those days. It was just that I was in such a frame of mind at that time it did not take much to upset me. I'm sure they understood.

I will always remember feeling terribly alone through all of this. I had been a decision-maker from way back. The decisions that had to be made at this time I handled well. It was just that there was never really anyone much to talk things over with. However, I look back with pride at the capable young woman I was in those times.

Even though the local priest and personal friend, Father Frank Williams, came to see Lyndy and me most nights, he could not really offer me any advice, just listen to my worries of the day. My dad, who we lived with at that time, would just say, "Oh don't worry, Tib, she'll be okay." Tib or Tiberta was the nickname Dad gave me when I was a small child. Cathy's own father said, "Just look how beautiful she looks. She will be okay."

This seems to be how it is with men, how they cope with these tragedies.

My mum had come from a large family and I remember her always being there for all of her brothers and sisters in times of trouble. Yet, Aunty Madge and Aunty Ella (two of Mum's sisters) came but once to see Cathy in all the time she was in hospital. Madge said, "I'm just glad Dot's not alive to see her little granddaughter sick like this. She would not have been able to bear seeing this."

"Oh well," I thought cynically, "at least someone has something to be glad about."

Oh what I would have given to have Mum there to support me. I needed her to comfort me so badly. I felt so alone. I have no recollection of my cousin Pattie or my brother Kenneth ever contacting me or going to the hospital to visit Cathy at that time.

I came home one night from the hospital. Lyndy was waiting at the door to greet me as usual. When I looked at her I was horrified as all her beautiful hair was gone, cut off really short! I mean short, short. We were once again back with the pixie cut.

"Whatever have you done to your hair?" I demanded. She said, "Now, Mum, sit down and let me explain." She had decided it was unfair on Cathy to have to look at her long hair when Cathy's hair had been shaved off, and it would be better if she had had all her hair cut off too.

At nine years old, I began to see the forming of her character as a real humanitarian, and many times over the years this side of her would shine through. We both ended up having a good cry to release some of our tension.

She shook her head and said, "Anyway, Mum, it feels good, so there."

Lyndy's hair had now been cut for the second time in her life. Cathy was directly involved on both occasions.

When they started chemotherapy on Cathy she had to stay in hospital all week, but could come home for the weekends. Every Sunday night Lyndy and I would take her back to hospital and we would both be an emotional mess, having to go home and leave Cathy behind at the hospital.

Lyndy and I were always upset and crying on our trip home along Victoria Road. It was an awful period in our lives. However, Cathy didn't seem to mind, as she would wave us off and settle into her hospital bed, chatting away to nurses and patients. She was such a brave little girl.

When Cathy was having chemotherapy I travelled to Camperdown every morning in time to accompany her in the hospital car to Prince of Wales Hospital in the city. I had the opportunity on these trips to study her files and try to get some understanding of what was happening to my little girl. In the 1960s the doctors were like gods. They never sat down and explained anything or volunteered information like they do today. My way of acquiring information about Cathy's condition was to sneak quick looks at her file. I wanted information about what was happening to her.

Cathy was sick and vomiting for a long time. Eventually her hair grew. However, there was a bald patch across the top of her head from the chemo so I bought her a partial wig. Thankfully her hair eventually grew back just as beautiful as ever.

Cathy was determined she would not be held back a class at school; she would sit up in bed with a sick bowl in one hand and a schoolbook in the other. Her mental strength held me in awe.

The prognosis could not have been worse. The doctors gave Cathy six months to live. They wanted to put a shunt in her brain. This is a device designed to drain away the excess fluid, that builds up in the brain due to the tumour. I had seen enough children with shunts in their brains. These children seemed to be forever in and out of hospital, having the shunts unblocked or replaced.

I was sitting with her one day when Doctor Jones came into the ward. He asked me to come to his rooms at three o'clock for a talk. That was a most dreaded day. He told me that there was no hope for Cathy, that she was going to die and he went on to describe in detail the terrible death she would have and how she would eventually lose the use of all her faculties.

There was nothing I could say to him. I asked him not one question. Some time later I was sitting on the gutter outside his rooms, in the grounds of Children's Hospital sobbing and vomiting. As I sat there I felt so alone, wondering how I could go back into the hospital and face my darling child. Suddenly I realised God had not deserted me completely. Walking towards me were Barbara Wood (the mother of Anne, Cathy's school friend) and Father Williams. Frank lifted me to my feet and hugged me to him as I sobbed and sobbed. I told them what had happened. I could not face Cathy I was such a mess. It was decided Barbara would go and spend some time with Cathy and Father Frank would take me home. I felt that for the first time ever I had failed Cathy, as I could not face her. However, I was back there the next morning ready to face another day.

After Cathy came home from hospital with this dreadful prognosis, I decided to take her to three different Macquarie Street neurosurgeons for their opinions and they all came up with much the same answers.

They all agreed with me and my gut feeling not to have any more surgery performed on her, to just leave her be.

However, they were all of the same opinion, they agreed with the hospital that Cathy's life expectancy was short. As one doctor said, "She is so beautiful, just let her be. Let her die without having any more operations." I must add none of these three surgeons would accept any payment from me for the advice they gave me.

It was coming up to Easter 1968 and the neurosurgeon who operated on Cathy had told me to take Cathy home for Easter and think about his advice to have a shunt inserted, and he warned me, "She would probably, I repeat probably (whatever 'probably' meant) be blind in six weeks without the shunt." I was told that there was only one other child in the world who had the same illness as Cathy had, and he had only lived as long as five years, however, now this child was like a vegetable.

I decided that that Easter would be as enjoyable as I could possibly make it, and it was. We had a wonderful happy Easter. However for the first time ever, we did not make our usual trip to the Sydney Royal Easter Show.

The six weeks were eventually up and Cathy was doing fine so I took her back to the children's hospital for a check-up. Lo and behold when we entered the lift the specialist who said Cathy would be blind within six weeks got in the lift behind us.

When he left the lift Cathy skipped ahead of him, did a little ballet pirouette in front of him and smiling up into his face said, "Good morning, Doctor Schreiber." When it came our turn to see the doctor we were taken into Doctor Jones. Needless to say Doctor Schreiber was avoiding me that morning.

I decided to take her out of all the medicos' hands, equipped only with my faith and Cathy's positive, happy outlook and deep-rooted, unbending faith in God, and the absolute devotion of her sister Lyndy and love of me, her mother. We faced the future bravely together.

The hospital did not wipe their hands of me entirely. They condescended to do tests monthly, three-monthly, six-monthly and then yearly check-ups to monitor her health. She was on Dilantin for the remainder of her life. Cathy never had an epileptic fit and rarely had a headache.

She went on to lead a normal life as a happy, healthy, well-adjusted child and teenager. She was gifted with her hands and did fine needlework. She made her own clothes, learnt ballet, ballroom dancing, elocution and swimming. However, it was a nightmare for me seeing her dive into the pool, but I had to come to the decision, "If Cathy dies living and doing these things, well at least she has lived. So be it." This was not an easy time for me. I had to continually stop myself from wrapping her in cotton wool.

Father Frank was always there and full of support while Cathy was in the hospital. I will never forget that he always had time and compassion for me in those painful days.

Father Frank came to see me one night. I remember saying to him, "Frank, if I can just have her for another 10 years?"

"I think it would be awful to lose a child at 18 years," he remarked.

I didn't agree. "I want to keep her as long as I can," I said.

My words would come back to haunt me, and I now know there is never an easy time to lose a child, no matter what age the child is.

Cathy having a day at home while having chemotherapy.

CHAPTER 10

THE BIRDS AND THE BEES

It was Christmas 1970. This was a good time in my life. I had finally thrown off the shackles of my overprotective parents. I was 34 years old and had virtually been single for about 10 years. Life was great. I loved my job teaching driving; I had a large circle of friends. It was a time of picnics at the beach every Sunday and always a party at someone's house every Saturday night.

I was at a party at my friend Ken Anderson's house one night, standing talking with a group of pals, when I looked across the room and saw a guy I had never seen before. I immediately felt drawn to him. It was an instant attraction. I remember looking at him and thinking "I'm going to marry him!" Then I thought, "June you must be mad! You've had enough of marriage."

I married Brian four months later. He was a short, ordinary-looking guy and not at all a happy type of person. I thought he was gorgeous! I had heard so much about chemistry from other women. How they could make their fortune if they could bottle and sell it. To me it had always been a load of nonsense, this chemistry thing. Then I met Brian and for the first time in my life I experienced chemistry! He was the man of my dreams. I finally found out what had been happening to that young woman in the next room to me, 15 years before when I was on my honeymoon with my first husband. I had 15 years to make up and we did just that. We had a 6 year honeymoon.

Mum had been dead for five years. If she had been still with me I could have said, "Hey, Mum, there is more to the 'facts of life' than the 'in and out thing' and having babies."

However, marriage to Brian was not a bed of roses He was an appalling nagger and obsessively jealous, and his jealousy caused many problems with my work, so I finally gave teaching driving away. The girls were having a private education and I had always been used to having plenty of money in my purse, so I decided to look for a job. I soon had an office position with F.T. Wimble at Rydalmere, in the very same street where Brian worked. As he travelled by public transport and I drove I always managed to be home before he was. I was working for several months before I decided I should break the news to him. Lyndy thought this was a riot. She would often whisper, "Don't forget to wave to him as you drive past, Mum."

Brian's mother came to stay for a few days. I decided to tell him I was working while she was with us. I really can't remember how I told him but I'm sure it would have been a very verbal weekend.

Good old Nan. I thought the world of her and she of me, but she was an old wretch. She often came to stay for a week and she would always put me out of my kitchen. That was no real problem as Nan was a wonderful cook. I always took the opportunity to relax with my *Daily Mirror* or a good book away from the slaving in the kitchen.

I was working again and happy. However, after a couple of years I found a job nearer to home with Carrier Air

Conditioning at Seven Hills. It was a job I absolutely loved. My duties incorporated banking (I mean thousands of dollars in my hand bag to be banked every morning), and every day a run into the City of Sydney in a company car. The City run was my favourite. I had to park in a parking station and walk the streets of Sydney; having executives sign documents for our company.

After living a single life for so many years, I found life with Brian extremely stressful and never became accustomed to his continual nagging. He would put sticky paper on the light switches, as we were all forever leaving the lights on. The girls and I would laugh at this, but it was stressful. It became a happy time on Saturday mornings when Brian went out and Lyndy and I would dance and sing around the house.

Possibly due to the stress of living with Brian, the migraine headaches I had suffered in the past returned. They were chronic. The doctor was always at our house giving me an injection for pain.

I had requested a referral to Professor Lance who worked out of the Prince Alfred Hospital at Camperdown. He had written a book and specialised in migraine headaches. The local doctor was reluctant to do this and I was desperate. One morning I went to the hospital and after explaining to the sister in charge what was happening to me, I asked to see Professor Lance.

"Oh no, you must have a referral," explained the sister at the desk. I persisted.

"I am going to sit on that chair over there, and if I have to sit there for a week I will. I'm not leaving until I have seen Professor Lance!"

After half an hour she came to me and said, "Professor Lance will see you now dear." He was a unique man, spoke in a soft cultured voice, and had sympathy for me. He devoted his life to research in his chosen field. I was admitted to hospital the very next day. They did everything to give me a migraine.

They gave me chocolates, cheese and even red wine. Nothing worked now I was in a peaceful environment, away from my own home.

I was in hospital for a week and he treated me with an extremely high dose of Sandomigran and instructed me to stand up to myself or to change my environment. The drug helped me a lot. I was eventually weaned off the drugs.

I returned home to life with Brian at our home in Doonside. I was a stronger person and I endeavoured to stand up to Brian more and be more assertive.

Lyndy was not sure she liked the new me! She had been reared to speak her mind and she often made a lot of sense despite her age.

When Cathy was 16 years old and was studying at Blacktown Secretarial College she met a local boy, Stephen Cain. This was the man she would eventually marry. Cathy worked at the Rural Bank at Seven Hills and later at the CBC Bank in George Street, Sydney, with Lyndy.

Cathy and Stephen were married on 24th January, 1976. Cathy was eighteen years old and Stephen was 23.

Lyndy was a human being with an enormous heart and she was everyone's friend. She was down to earth. She always had a lot to say. This was the cause of a lot of problems at school. She was too hard for the nuns on many occasions.

Like her father she had a great gift for drawing. She had a multitude of friends of all ages, from 10-year-old kids to very old people. I saw her as a complete humanitarian and extrovert. She adored her sister and spent her free time mostly with Cathy or me.

If someone was down and out Lyndy was always there for him or her.

When Lyndy left school she went nursing at Prince Henry Hospital, but not for long though. She loved taking care of people, but she was too soft-hearted and really not robust enough for the life. Lyndy would go to visit some of her patients on her days off.

She started working at CBC Bank in Martin Place in Sydney, but she was not happy until Cathy was working there with her. Daily they travelled to work together with Angela Larkin, Lyndy's long-time, best friend.

When Cathy turned 17 years old she wanted to learn to drive. While everyone in the family had grave fears of Cathy ever being behind the wheel of a car, she was intrepid about the whole thing. That was Cathy.

My husband Brian's first words were, "She'll run up the back of someone looking at herself in the mirror!"

Of course I got on the defensive and said, "How would you know, you don't even drive yourself."

Since I had taught driving for 14 years, I was the obvious one to take on this onerous task. We soon found out that this was not a good idea. Then Stephen, her future husband, decided it was not a good idea for him to teach her either. So, it was off to the driving school for Cathy to have some lessons.

Finally, she went for her driver's licence, and of course being Cathy, she passed her test the first time. How, I'll never know.

"You see, Mum, I told you I could do it. Now I need to buy a car, seeing I can drive," she exclaimed. I did not feel one bit confident about any of this.

Stephen thought the sun shone out of our Cathy and of course he said she could have his car any time.

The thought of Cathy behind the wheel of Stephen's car horrified me.

Stephen's car at that time was a Ford Fairlane V8, would you believe? Cathy, all 4 foot 10 inches of her, had no qualms. However, the rest of the family sure were worried.

One afternoon, Nan was standing at my kitchen window looking out. "Oh! Oh! Dear God, there's a big, white car coming around the corner without a driver," she cried.

Nan was spooked out of her mind!

Cathy was so tiny; she had to drive by looking through the steering wheel.

One day she was driving up a hill at Quakers Hill and ran up the back of a big truck. She told me later, "Mummy, it was the fault of Stephen's car, it stalled!"

"I sat there crying and this big, burly truck driver came up to the car, opened the door, and drove to the side of the road. He turned off the engine and jumped out of the car and closed the door. Would you believe he didn't even have the manners to ask if I was okay? He just shook his head and walked off. I really just can't understand men," she told me.

"Oh well," I said to Lyndy, "at least we won't have to worry about her driving Stephen's car again." This was not so. The very next day she pulled up out the front of our house in Stephen's Ford Fairlane again.

"Oh Mummy, you just worry too much," she remarked.

Stephen had to really love this little girl of mine. I mean really, unconditionally, love her. Cathy had saved up $600. So she and Stephen set off one Saturday morning to look for a car for her.

A few days later after much searching they arrived home, both as happy as can be. They had purchased her new car. "I had just enough money," she said.

The car was a Mini Cooper S.

I had no idea what a Mini Cooper S was. It just looked like another Mini to me.

"Oh well, surely she can't get into too much trouble with a Mini," I thought.

About three days after Cathy purchased her Mini, I received a phone call from some guy. "I wish to speak to Cathy Stiles' mother," he demanded in an officious voice.

"Speaking," I replied as he carried on.

"Are you aware your daughter is driving a car she has stolen?"

"And who might you be?" I said. My temper was in

full swing immediately.

"I'm the salesman from the car yard. I sold your daughter a Mini, and she stole a Mini Cooper S from our yard. She has 24 hours to return the car or we will call in the police!" I promptly hung up on him. I'd never been so angry.

I rang Stephen at work, and then I went off to the local police station to make my complaint against this company. The long and the short of this mess was, Cathy and Stephen test-drove a Mini, and a Mini Cooper S. Then they decided between the two of them to settle on the Cooper S. They inquired on the price and were given the price of the Mini.

Stephen said, "Gee, Cath, that's a good price, you should take it!"

The two cars were both cream in colour and they had almost identical number plates. To top the whole thing off, the salesman wrote them a receipt, and inadvertently gave them the keys to the Cooper S, so away they drove.

What a mess! Well I finally sorted the whole thing out. I threatened the guy with defamation of character and whatever else I could think of.

We ended up paying them the extra money and Cathy got to keep the Cooper S.

After she married Stephen, she decided to sell the car to a girl I worked with and she made a profit! It was "Unheard of, to sell a second-hand car and make a profit. Typical of Cathy!" Lyndy pointed out.

That car was the worry of my life. Every Thursday night she would say, "Come on, Mummy, I'll take you shopping."

I always came home sick in the stomach.

One Thursday she ran up the back of another car, and then on the next corner she ran up the back of the same car again. Oh God, I was a nervous wreck. Fortunately, there was no real damage incurred. All Cathy could say was, "Well, why does she keep stopping?" shaking her beautiful blonde head, not one bit perturbed.

At this time Cathy was working at the Rural Bank at Seven Hills. The bank was on a very busy road, so I would follow her each morning on my way to work. "At least I know she is getting to work safely." I thought.

I said to her one day, "Darling, how do you ever get out of work in the afternoon, in peak hour, and having to make a right-hand turn across the traffic?"

"Oh, there's no problem, Mummy, I just sit there and some nice man always seems to turn up and stop the traffic for me, so I can turn for home; so don't start worrying about that now," she said.

I guess being blonde with big, blue eyes and beautifully helpless came in handy.

These things never seemed to happen to me.

It was a happy day for me when the Cooper S was sold.

CHAPTER 11

CATHY'S WEDDING

Cathy and Stephen had been going together for a couple of years and they wanted to become engaged. As much as we all loved Stephen, I thought she was too young. However, after a lot of nagging and promises that they would not marry for years, I agreed to an engagement.

We had a large party at home, which gave us the chance to meet all of Stephen's relatives.

Stephen's family were a very close-knit clan and as we got to know them we came to love spending time with them.

Nan came and stayed with us for a week and she took control of the cooking and preparations. Nan wasn't one for fancy words or endearments, but I felt she loved us all very much.

Within months of becoming engaged Cathy and Steve were making plans to get married.

I spoke to Dr Christie, our family physician, as I still harboured doubts about Cathy being married at such a young age, particularly with all her health problems. I was not sure she could handle the responsibility of married life.

Dr Christie felt they should go ahead with their plans.

"June," he said "let her grasp whatever happiness she can while she can."

Dr Christie always saw Cathy as having a short life expectancy. I never did see her in that way. I always remained positive of her having a long life ahead of her.

I had to think this way.

The first step in their plans was to pay Father Frank a visit. Frank was now the parish priest at Wyong on the North Coast and Cathy was sure he would come to Parramatta to perform their nuptials for them.

Frank's reaction to Cathy and Stephen's plans was a devastating shock to us all.

Frank (much to his regret) refused to marry Cathy and Stephen. Due to Cathy's history of illness we had been informed that she should never fall pregnant, as the risk of a relapse rose greatly during pregnancy. Frank saw marriage as a child-bearing contract, and as Cathy could not have children she could not marry in the Catholic Church.

Frank's beliefs in his teachings overrode his love for Cathy and our family.

Cathy was the third generation of women in our family to be told that she could not have children. First my mother, then me, then Cathy.

Everyone was angry with Frank. I wasn't. I realised that he was following the Church's instructions and I did not hold his decision against him. He had been too good to me over all the years of Cathy's illness. Some years earlier there were problems between Cathy and Stephen. Cathy, I felt, was trying to convert Stephen to Catholicism. As much as he loved her he had strong convictions. He is an atheist and could never say he believed when he didn't.

Cathy's beliefs were important to her, and she had followed her faith with such strong conviction since her first day at school.

The romance became a real soap opera. Cathy had broken it off with Stephen and said she would not see him any more.

Stephen would still come through the kitchen door every night. Lyndy would make him his coffee (she had her own agenda) and Cathy would all but ignore him.

It was a riot. He would go and sit in the lounge room as if nothing had changed. Cathy would be speaking to him in a whisper and Lyndy would be popping from one room to the other relaying anything she heard to me.

Lyndy was having fun and one night she whispered to me in all seriousness, "Mum, if Cathy doesn't want Stephen he may like to take me out!"

Before I could say anything to her she was in there putting her proposition to him.

Stephen kindly turned to her and said, "Maybe in time, Lyndy, you are a little young for me just yet." She accepted this quite amicably.

Stephen kept coming every night; he was not going to give up on his Cathy.

A lot of whispering was still taking place, and suddenly, somehow, he was back with us and they were making wedding plans again.

I held Stephen in high esteem for taking a stand even though it meant they would have to marry outside the Catholic Church.

Cathy's health was never an issue with him. His love for Cathy ran too deep for anything to interfere.

After months of pattern-making, sewing, altered ideas and tears I had finally finished making Cathy's wedding dress, Lyndy's bridesmaid dress, the bouquets and headdresses.

The big day was fast approaching and I realised I would not have time to make an outfit for myself. My outfit was shop made.

Their wedding day finally came and my girls looked

beautiful. Cathy and Stephen were married in the Church of England in Blacktown.

The reception was held at home. Nan was in control as usual, but we kept her out of the kitchen and hired caterers and waiters.

Cathy and Stephen had their honeymoon and then went to live in our old home at 66 Victoria Road, Parramatta.

The months slipped by, but Cathy's happiness was not quite complete. She was attending Mass every Sunday, but she could not take the sacraments.

This devastated Cathy and one Sunday after Mass she was sitting in Prince Alfred Park having a cry about her situation with the Church. It was affecting her much more than she had expected.

The parish had recently acquired a new, young priest whose name was Father Mark.

Just at this moment Father Mark was taking a stroll through the park to contemplate, as he often did after he had said a Mass.

As he strolled along he glanced to his right and saw this pretty young woman sitting on a park bench. Mark knew her by sight; he had seen this tiny girl with the long blonde hair in church and around the parish several times. He decided to approach her.

Suddenly Cathy realised the young priest was sitting beside her. He took her hand and asked what her tears were all about.

After a long chat Father Mark knew all of Cathy's troubles. He thought about all this for a time.

He then told her they would need to wait six months from their wedding day on 24th January and then her would marry her on 24th July, 1976 in her own church.

We asked no questions of Mark, we were all too happy to see Cathy's happiness complete.

Father Mark became a great friend to Cathy and Stephen

and many a night he sat down to dinner with them and survived Cathy's cooking.

Unfortunately, Father Mark could not come to terms with life and met a tragic end. The death in the train of the girls and so many other young people in the parish were all too much for Mark.

Cathy's Wedding Day

CHAPTER 12

MY SPECIAL CHILD

Brian often remarked to me. "You are like three peas in a pod. Is there room for a fourth pea in your pod?"I would sit on the lounge to read my beloved *Daily Mirror.* Brian would be on one side of me, Lyndy the other. I would be having a bath and Brian would come in and sit on the stool to talk to me. Lyndy would be knocking on the door. Did I ever feel crowded out? Never! I loved it all.

We were so close, I know now that Cathy would have survived Lyndy's death. Lyndy would never have survived Cathy's death. I have survived the death of Cathy and Lyndy. The pain – I am thankful in some way that it is my pain and not theirs. Better for me to have suffered the loss of them than them to have suffered the loss of me or be forced to survive the one without the other. Psychics and the like have told me over the years that the girls' souls are earthbound. I am always left with a feeling of guilt. I could never seem to cut the tie and let them go. How could I when my heart had been torn apart?

Over the years I have asked many people, men and women,

"Do you have a special child?" Rarely was anyone to answer "Yes!"

It has generally been, "No, I love all my children equally."

I believe if they had the courage, at least some of them would have said "Yes."

I'm sure I treated Cathy and Lyndy equally in every way. I loved both of them with all my heart!

However, Lyndy always held a place deep down in my heart and still does. A special, unique place!

Yes, I did love Lyndy more than any other person who has been in my life.

Was it because she was born on my birthday?

Was it because she was my rebel?

We loved more, hugged more, laughed more and we argued more!

I remember one day she said, "You know, Mum, you would have to have last say, even if you made a stupid statement!" And that just about summed it up.

I did always have to have last say, and more so when I was younger. Perhaps I have mellowed somewhat now.

Well the three of us were like sisters. Maybe this was because I was so young when the girls were born.

Lyndy and I possibly bonded even more during and after Cathy's fight with brain cancer. During this time of great trauma, as young as she was, Lyndy was a source of great strength to me. This special child of mine.

It must have been traumatic for Lyndy, as she was so young when Cathy contracted the brain tumour. I often wondered how aware she was of Cathy's terrible illness and possible early death.

When Cathy became ill Lyndy became the family doctor. She spent hours poring over medical dictionaries. She was forever at the library looking for information. She came to me in a panic one day. Cathy had told her she had one breast larger than the other. Lyndy was worried, in a panic that the cancer had spread to her breast. We immediately made an appointment to see Doctor Christie. He examined Cathy and turned to me and said, "June, get rid of those medical dictionaries out of the house. Lyndy is worse than the bloody local chemist." Lyndy was all of nine years old.

Seven years after Cathy had been diagnosed with a brain tumour, Lyndy began nagging me, "Mum, it's time we had a serious talk about Cathy's health."

"Well," I said to her one day, "We will get your exams over first, and then we will have a week's holiday up north together, just the two of us, somewhere by the sea." This was something we did occasionally, Lyndy and me. We usually went to Manly and stayed at Eversham, a private hotel almost on the beach.

Lyndy's final exams were around the same time as her 16th birthday. She was working very hard. "I have to get better marks than Cathy and Stephen," she told me. Her sister and stepbrother both found studying much easier than she did. Lyndy studied very hard for those exams, every minute she studied. When her results came out she had done extremely well, and was over the moon with happiness. Ecstatic.

Once she finished we went on our holiday.

It was a special time for Lyndy and myself, and I have many treasured memories of those days. Lyndy had a gap in her life now that Cathy was spending so much time with Stephen. I knew she was lonely for her sister at times.

When November came we set off up the North Coast highway and the first stop was to see Nan, Brian's mother, at Berkley Vale. Now Nan had always been a good cook, and she piled up our car with food, including a large mulberry pie.

Nan's mulberry pies were something to die for! She was a bit of an old terror, but I loved her. She often came to stay with us for a week, and she would ban me from my own kitchen.

Nan and I had never had a cross word.

Lyndy and I found a small unit on the water's edge at Nelson Bay. "This is the life for me," she declared. Now my idea of a perfect holiday had always been to stay up late and sleep in late, but this was not to be on this particular holiday. At the break of dawn the next morning Lyndy woke me. "Mum," she said, "One thing you have to do before you die is watch the sunrise over the water."

Never would I have imagined that this would possibly be the last time Lyndy would see a sunrise. There we were at 4.30am, down on the water's edge, waiting for the sun to come up, and it did itself justice; it was a spectacularly beautiful sunrise. It was just a wonderful event in my life, to be there in that wondrous place, with this beautiful, spiritual, child-teenager-young woman, daughter of mine. We were seeing this spectacular sunrise for our first and last time together. I have never again had the desire to watch a sunrise. We sat there on the beach for an age.

Finally, she said, "Come on, old girl, how about a long walk on the beach?" We walked the full length of that beach in silence with the water lapping at our ankles. Suddenly we came upon the strangest sight. There, in front of us, were at least two dozen men, lined up, one behind the other on the beach. They reminded me of little tin soldiers.

"Whatever can they be doing, Lyn?" I asked.

"You never know, my girl, they could be out waiting to meet someone, maybe me or perhaps even you?" We continued on our walk and on our return we found the answer. These guys were waiting for a fishing trawler to pick them up for a day's deep-sea fishing, and so this was their reason for the early morning line-up.

Our week together was just wonderful. It was something for me to store away among my treasury of memories to cherish for ever. On the first evening of our holiday we went for a drive and parked by the water to watch the surf break over the sand. We had a long talk about Cathy's health and the fact that her future was not good, not at all promising. I explained to her that her sister did not have a great life expectancy, and about how I had made the decision to let her live her life as if everything was normal; however, the doctors had informed us that Cathy should never fall pregnant, as child-bearing could start the brain tumour growing again. So all we could ever do was live one day at a time. I didn't hide anything from her as she wanted to know everything, and I decided that at the age of 16, she was mature enough to cope. Lyndy handled it all with wisdom beyond her years and I was really very proud of her. Her response was, we will have to just love her, take life one day at a time, and trust that God leaves her with us, and she is healthy for a long, long time.

Lyndy was a brave young girl. She adored her sister and seemed to take it all fairly much in her stride. I'm sure I would not have been brave if I had known at that time that both my girls had just two years left on this earth.

The next evening, around 8.30 we had had our dinner and were getting ready to tuck into Nan's mulberry pie.

It had started raining and for the past half an hour it had fallen down in sheets. Lyndy said "Gee, Mum, I love the rain when I'm tucked up in the warmth with a good book."

Suddenly there was loud banging on the front door. "For god's sake, who could that be at our door at this time of night?" I demanded. Lyndy hopped up and went to answer the door. There was a woman of about 60 standing there dripping wet.

"Could I please come in? I need somewhere to stay the night. My car has broken down, the phones are all out and the roads are cut," she said.

"Sure," says Lyndy. "Come right in, Mum will make up a bed for you, no trouble at all." That was my Lyndy, everyone's friend. And what a strange night it turned out to be! First, the three of us tackled Nan's mulberry pie. By the time we had eaten it, I might add, we were all feeling very sick.

Lyndy, myself and our new-found friend sat around the kitchen table laughing and joking as if we had known each other for years. Unfortunately I don't remember our guest's name. She lived in a large house overlooking the water at Salamander Bay and I guess she has passed on by now. Who knows, she may be up above eating mulberry pie with my Lyndy? I will call her Joanne.

Joanne looked at me and said, "I'm sure I know your face!"

And I replied, "Yes, Joanne, and I know your face from somewhere also." She smiled at me and asked did I ever shop in Parramatta? "Parramatta! I was born at Granville, and I spent all my working years at Parramatta," I said.

Joanne then told me she had owned a women's accessories shop in Church Street, Parramatta, some 20 odd years before and that she could remember me coming in with my silk stockings, to have their ladders mended, when I was a young girl.

It's a very small world sometimes.

Now I was faced with the problem of where we were going to bed down our guest in this tiny flat? The only option was to make her a bed on the lounge, and we were soon all fast asleep. The next morning we all tucked into bacon and eggs, and then Joanne set off to find a phone and ring her probably frantic husband to hand her car problems over to.

The holiday was soon over and we headed off home down the coast highway. On the way home we called into Berkley Vale for a cuppa with Nan. She had hot scones waiting for us. Suddenly Lyndy said, "Nan, can I have a look through your wardrobe, I need something?"

Nan and I sat there chatting and Lyndy came out with this great heavy overcoat. Nan was a big, tall woman and we both started to laugh. The coat was large enough for three of her. "Now, Nan, you won't be going to Tasmania any more and this is just what I'm looking for!"

The mystery finally unfolded. Lyndy had a friend she met on the train going to work. This lady was rearing her three grandchildren and she was always cold, but could not afford an overcoat for herself.

I felt proud I had put such a beautiful young woman out there.

Two years later we were coming up to Christmas again, Christmas 1976, and there were two dramas happening with Lyndy and myself.

The first was the Christmas tree. "Mumsy, let's get a new Christmas tree, this old thing is disgusting. I would love a large white tree, white with pink bows, yes, pretty pink bows!"

"No," I laughed at her. "I refuse to buy a new tree until I have my first granddaughter. No pink bows until she eventually comes along," I laughed. The doctors had said Cathy should never conceive a child so I told Lyndy it was up to her to give me my granddaughter. Never could I have known in those deliriously happy days that I would never have the thrill of holding a grandchild.

Now to the second drama. Cathy knew she was getting a new Seiko watch from Stephen for Christmas, and Lyndy was pushing me to buy a Seiko for her. I told her if she gave up smoking (a bone of contention between us) I would buy her a Seiko.

As Christmas was fast approaching the tension was running high in our household. Every night Lyndy would come in from work and go straight to the Christmas tree to feel all the presents under the tree. She was feeling for the Seiko. It was the 23rd December and she was persisting. "Mumsy, what's happening about the Seiko?"

"Have you given up smoking?" I asked.

"Have you seen me smoking?" she retorted, with a cheeky grin on her face.

The bantering continued. I felt sure she had not given up smoking!

I later whispered to Brian, "I'm going to buy her a Seiko tomorrow!" Brian then proceeded to tell me how spoilt she was. Of course his objections helped me make up my mind; I was going to buy it for her.

And how much I would have regretted it if I had chosen not to buy the Seiko for Lyndy, on what was to be my last Christmas with her. The last time we would put up our Christmas tree together. There would never be the white Christmas tree with pretty pink bows.

In all her years at school Lyndy did not have a great deal of time for the nuns. However, she adored her two lay teachersm Miss Anne Dobler and Miss Eckersley. Miss Dobler phoned me one day and said Lyndy had called to see her a short time before her untimely death. She had called to show Miss Dobler her lovely new car. She was so proud of the little red 1969 Ford Capri.

Anne Dobler related to me that as Lyndy was leaving her home she had said to her, "Now you be careful driving that car, Lyndy… No speeding!"

Lyndy had turned to her and tossing her hair and laughing she said, "Dobe, when your time comes… it comes."

I guess Anne Dobler felt the need to pass on this last fragment of our Lyndy to me…

When Lyndy was attending college it always bugged her that the college building needed painting. She was forever saying to me, "I don't know, Mum, all the thousands they receive in school fees. They are too mean to buy some paint."

A short time after Lyndy died I was driving past the college when I noticed it had been painted. I stopped my car and sat there thinking, "Oh, Lyndy will be so happy when I tell her they have painted the school building at last."

For a split second I had forgotten I didn't have her with me any more.

I started to cry… devastated all over again.

Lyndy visits Ann Doubler in her new Ford Capri

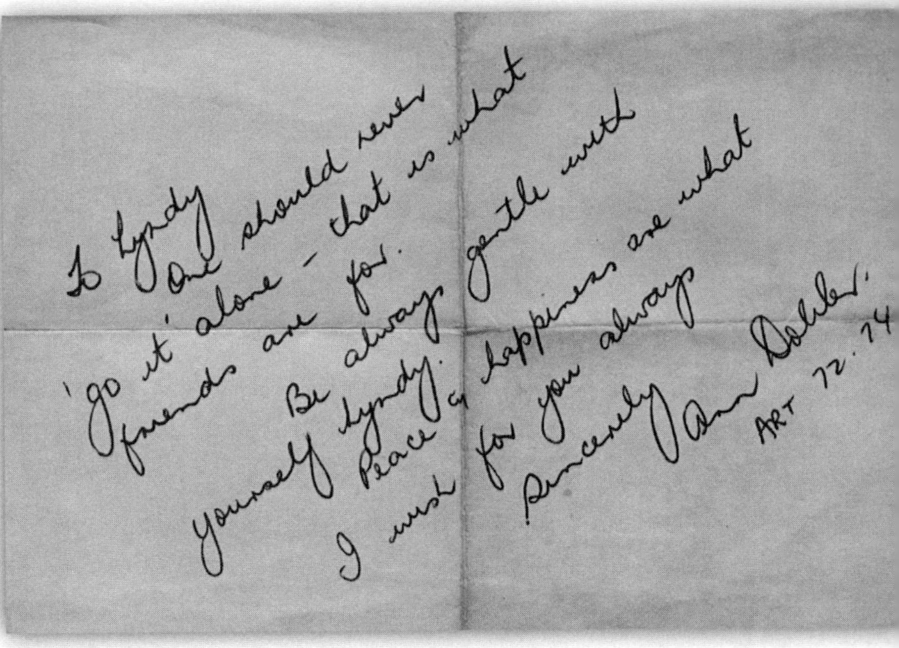

To Lyndy
One should never
'go it' alone – that is what
friends are for.
Be always gentle with
yourself Lyndy.
Peace & happiness are what
I wish for you always
Sincerely
Ann Dobler.
ART 72.74

Notes From Ann I found in her wallet.

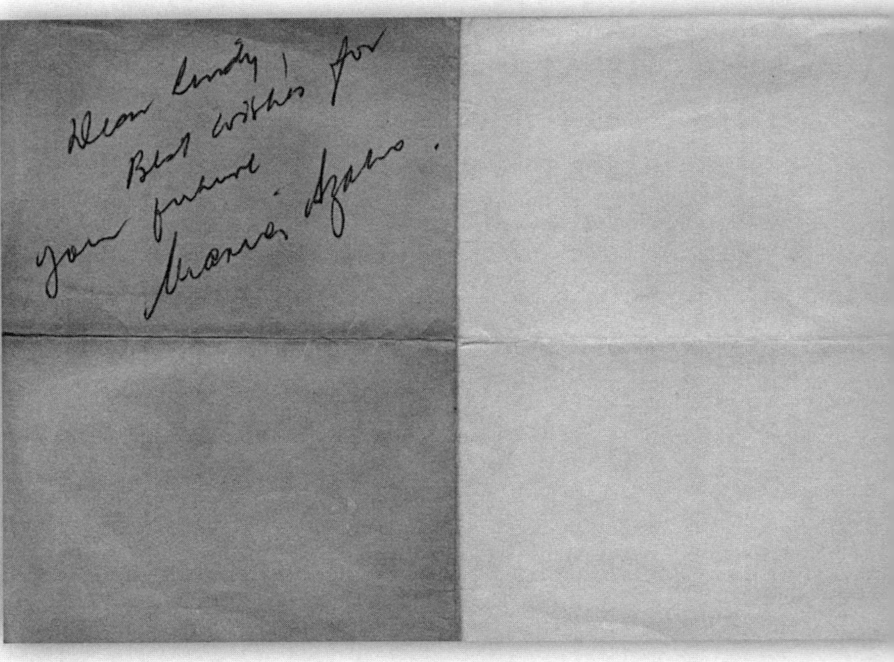

Dear Lindy,
Best wishes for
your future
Maria Szabo.

CHAPTER 13

NO TOMORROWS

In January 1977 Brian and I had planned a holiday to treat ourselves. We had arranged to stay at a lovely guesthouse at The Entrance on the North Coast of NSW for a couple of weeks. I had never left either of the girls alone before. I was concerned about leaving Lyndy alone at home but had relaxed a little when Steven, Brian's son, had agreed to come back home for a couple of weeks to be there with my Lyndy in the evenings.

By mid-morning, Brian and I had arrived at The Entrance for our romantic, week-long break away from the children. Our room at the guesthouse more than met our expectations. "The fishing should be good," said Brian. Well the fishing may have been good; I only ever saw fish once! I would drop him off some days at his favourite fishing spot and call back later for him. Hours later, there he would be, still in the same place, happy as ever. Sometimes I would take a book, sit beside him and read. Brian was never a patient man, but with fishing he had the patience of a saint! Fishing did not interest me in those days, yet many years later, while living in Perth, to my surprise, I became quite an accomplished deep-sea fisherwoman.

We had been away just over a week. I had been calling the girls on alternate nights, Cathy one night, Lyndy the next. They were both fine.

The morning of the 18th January dawned bright and sunny. We rose early. Brian felt today was the day he would bring home a swagful of fish. I resisted teasing him about feeding all the other guests for dinner. Just before we set off, I decided to go to the post office and ring the girls at the bank. They should have been at work by then. I couldn't raise either of them last night, so I felt a bit concerned. I didn't know why.

"Oh they're okay," said Brian. "You're always worrying about them."

Nevertheless, I ran off with some coins in my hand. "No sorry, neither Cathy nor Lyndy are in as yet," said the girl on the switchboard at the bank. "That's strange" I thought, "they must both be having a day off. Oh well, I'll call home and see what's going on." I phoned home, but there was no answer, so I phoned Cathy and Stephen's home at Parramatta. The lines were down. The mystery deepened.

I was puzzled as I set off back to the guesthouse.

When I got back Brian was ready to take off for fishing for the day, naturally getting impatient. "Come on," he insisted, "The day will be over before we get there!"

I felt a bit uneasy. However, I went with him.

We arrived back just after lunch and there was a message for us to phone Brian's mother. Nan relayed the news – there had been a train disaster in Sydney. The boys – Cathy's husband, Stephen, and Brian's son, Steven – had been trying to contact us. I remember running down the street to the public phone. Hysterical, I dropped my money. A lady picked it up for me. She grabbed my hand and asked if she could help. I brushed her aside and kept running.

I finally reached a public phone at the post office and

phoned my mother-in law. She must have been sitting by the phone. Nan answered the phone on the first ring. “Yes,” she said, “things look bad. The boys, Stephen and Steven, have been phoning all morning. You must come home quickly! Cathy and Lyndy could have been on that train.” Nan was distraught.

By the time I arrived back at the guesthouse June and Burt (Brian’s cousins) were there, waiting to take us to Sydney. They knew it would not be a good idea for me to drive, as they had anticipated my state of mind.

I remember distinctly, while travelling back to Parramatta, turning to Brian and saying, “Brian, if anything has happened to the girls, I am finished with you. You refused to have children with me. You have taken my future away from me.” I must have been so full of fear and bitterness; someone had to take the blame, bear the brunt of my anger. In retrospect, he did not deserve this cruel treatment. I vented my hurt and fear on him.

It flashed through my mind … No children. No grandchildren. No white Christmas trees with pink bows. No tomorrows.

We arrived back in Sydney in the early afternoon. The two boys were at Cathy and Stephen’s house in Parramatta. Everything was in a state of chaos.

Sydney was in shock! All of Australia was in shock. This catastrophe was being flashed around the world.

The decision was made for Brian and I to return to Doonside, further up the rail line to where we lived. The boys would wait at Parramatta, just in case the girls, somehow, came home.

CHAPTER 14

IN RETROSPECT

In the 1970s in Australia our world had never been touched by terrorism, train crashes or major disasters.The Granville Train Disaster stunned our world. On 18 January, 1977 the whole of the Western Suburbs of Sydney was thrown into shock and chaos. We were confronted with our first major disaster. Our first catastrophic train disaster was upon us.

We were totally unprepared. There was not even a SEC in place. Granville was in total chaos.

Not just Granville, but the whole of the west, right up through the Blue Mountains, through to the whole of Sydney, Australia and even overseas, everyone, like myself, was trying to ring home, to friends and relatives. Were they okay? Were they involved? Almost everyone in Sydney, at least, was somehow connected to this disaster. They could have lost a loved one, a friend. Thousands of people left their place of work. They just walked away. Nothing mattered except to find that their loved ones were safe. People either headed for home or to the scene. The Salvation Army was there, but the police were sending people away; they were a hindrance.

The phone lines crashed. They could not take this overload from desperate people.

I could not get through to Steven. I had to travel by car from the North Coast. Cathy and Lyndy's father, John, drove up from Wollongong and stayed at the scene for two days waiting for news.

Some time later I met up with a friend. She said she was in London on that day. "God," she said, "You could spot the Aussies on the streets of London that day. We were all running around hysterical, crying and trying to get through to Australia.

"We were queuing up at public phones and trying to buy newspapers. Looking for lists of the dead or injured. Strangers were hugging strangers. We were all trying to comfort each other."

Immediately upon arriving home, I set myself up by the phone. My organising skills had come to the fore.

"Operation Find My Girls and Have Them Home Again" had begun. I made a list of every hospital in Sydney, phoned them, gave a description of the girls, what they were wearing, etc. I was on the phone all that Tuesday, all that night and the following morning, ringing and re-ringing hospitals and the police. No-one had any answers for me. I felt Brian let me down badly. He went to bed and left me. However, Steven, who had come home earlier when there was still no sign of the girls, lay at my feet most of the night. I really had no conception of what the chaos was like at Granville. I just couldn't understand where the girls were and why they had not come home.

It seems ironic our television was never switched on over this period of time. I often ponder on the cathartic value of the visual and other media coverage had we thought to avail ourselves of it in those crucial days. At a time like this, human beings deal with such trauma in their own unique ways.

The enormity of what had taken place at Granville never

entered my mind and therefore was never a part of my reality. Instead I chose to take on a fugue state in which part of my brain shut down in order to protect my sanity.

In this state I could go on believing that my girls would be coming home. I was trying to protect myself. In retrospect, I know this was not a good decision for me.

After many hours on the phone, ringing hospitals and the police, I still had no answers. Eventually, a sergeant of police was assigned to me to help find the girls.

At around 10am on Wednesday, 19th January, 1977, 26 hours after the disaster had taken place, I was looking out the front window in complete despair. A very young police constable was walking up my front path. He had come to tell me my Lyndy, my younger daughter, my lovely, 18 year-old child, had been identified as a fatality in the Granville Train Disaster. I cannot account for the next few hours. I was completely numb. I walked around my home in a trance.

The life of this lovely young girl was over! Over before it had really begun.

I really don't know what transpired after that. What the young policeman said I have no idea. Just that she was gone and there was no news of my Cathy as yet. Angela Larkin, Lyndy's best friend right through school, was also missing.

26 hours after this dreadful disaster, no-one could tell me where my Cathy was. "It's possible she is in shock, has wandered off somewhere." they tried to reassure me.

Cathy was not identified until the next day. She had been taken too. I may have been in that fugue state at this time, as I have no recollection of being informed of Cathy's death.

It was inconceivable that both my precious girls, my only children, were dead. They had lost their lives in this catastrophic train disaster. They had been taken away from me for ever! I felt stunned and immobilised…

I recall phoning Father Frank and asking him to come down to Sydney to identify the girls for me. Frank was at this time the Parish Priest of Wyong on the Central Coast of NSW.

I recall at that time that Frank was very disturbed and distant with me on the phone. He went home to Wyong without coming to see me. I only found out in 2008 that when Frank arrived at the morgue that had been set up at Granville, Les Cain was there to identify the girls, and an awful altercation took place. According to my friend Ian Mitchell, Les Cain (Stephen's brother) had turned to Father Frank then and there and said, "So you have come to bury Cathy have you? Yet you would not fucking marry her in your church would you!" I was shocked to hear this after all these years, yet I could understand Les reacting in this way. The Cains all loved Cathy dearly and had been very disturbed the year before when Frank had said she could not be married in the Catholic Church because she would never be able to bear a child due to her illness.

Several months after the girls died I was visiting Stephen, and his brother Les was there. I started questioning him "Were you sure about the identification of the girls?" I don't recall the exact conversation, but he told me he was certain about Cathy, and yet he hesitated when I asked him about Lyndy. He seemed to become quiet and there was something odd, I thought. He remarked about how sometimes it's hard to tell when you identify a dead person.

I now know that that was the very moment, when Les Cain made that statement, that the first real seed of doubt was sown.

I mistook what he was trying to tell me. In that split second in time, and because my brain could not face the reality of this dreadful tragedy, I grabbed on to this false thread of hope.

That day set me on a pattern of thinking that would stay with me for many years.

It is only now that I realise that that day Les was trying to tell me, "Lyndy was crushed, probably beyond recognition."

I wonder now, would this knowledge at that time have helped in my healing process or would it have completely pushed me over the edge.

At least now, 30 odd years on, hopefully I am mentally and emotionally strong enough to live with this dreadful reality.

For many years after Lyndy died, maybe 10 or even longer, there were periods of time when I would feel sure she was still alive! I would be walking in a busy street and be sure I had caught a glimpse of her in the distance.

How often I ran up to a young woman with long hair flowing down her back only to be again disappointed… She did not have my Lyndy's face.

I lived for years off and on with the thought that maybe she wandered away from the scene of the train disaster and lost her memory.

I never did find her on the streets of Sydney, Perth, Queensland or anywhere else in the world.

I'm not sure when these delusions stopped, many years ago I guess, or maybe I just gave up.

CHAPTER 15

TWO WHITE COFFINS

A week later, on 24th January 1977, my girls were buried. I only vaguely recall the presence of relatives and friends in the house over that first dreadful week. However, I do remember feeling numb. I don't recall crying, just this stunned, lonely numbness as I moved about my home. I did not cry at all over this whole period of time in my life.

One morning during that dreadful week, I imagined Lyndy's alarm went off. I jumped out of bed and went to her bedroom door and said, "Lyndy, turn that alarm off, it will wake everyone!" – Lyndy was always in trouble over that damned alarm – Oh my God, I realised her bed was empty! I stood there looking at the empty bed. I would never see her cheeky face smiling at me again. The dam burst! For the first time I faced this terrible reality. I would never see my darling, beautiful child again.

Another day during that week, I glanced out the back window. Stephen was coming up the path. I instinctively looked past him, wondering "Where's Cathy?" Then the realisation hit me, Stephen would never walk up my path with Cathy ever again. I felt devastated and shattered. I had always known when Cathy would be home. I always heard her laughing before I saw her coming. After she met Stephen her laughter took on a lyrical, tinkling, bell-like sound. It was the sound of a woman in love.

The local priest came to see me. "Did Lyndy go to Mass on Sunday?" he inquired.

"What in God's name did it matter?" I shouted. I had lost it. My composure was gone.

I was shaking violently and screamed at him in rage. My daughters were dead and all he cared about was whether or not Lyndy had gone to Mass on Sunday. The priest retreated and I never saw him again.

Doctor Brian Carney came out to the house a few days later. He had been a resident at the Camperdown Children's Hospital where I had taken Cathy 10 years earlier. He went on to become Superintendent of the Children's Hospital, and Cathy often saw him at Mass after she was married. He was stunned over the death of the girls. I distinctly remember thinking, "What strange behaviour for a doctor? He should be able to cope with this; he sees death all the time." yet he broke down. Doctor Carney had been away and had just that day heard the news of the girls' death. I know now he was terribly distressed and acting instinctively. He had just been told that Cathy, his patient of 10 years earlier, had been so tragically taken. It was beyond his comprehension. In his distress he spoke about how I had taken Cathy out of the hands of the hospital and in so doing I had possibly saved her life at that time.

I now realise that I was in shock. It was me who was not acting rationally. I carried on in this fugue state doing my chores, talking to people. I had certainly not come to terms with the death of my two girls.

In that week following the death of the girls the government sent a psychologist to see me. Grief counselling was unheard of in those days and she was obviously way out of her depth. I was in deep shock and denial and she did not realise this.

She had barely been in the house 10 minutes when she stated flippantly, "Well I can see you're okay. You don't need any help, you're coping well." Then she left.

Thankfully, that kind of attitude would not be acceptable in these enlightened days.

We have become more aware and responsible over the past 30 years, surely.

Today, grief counselling is an accepted everyday occurrence in times of tragedy.

I have often thought in the years that have passed that if I had had some real help in those early days my life may have been easier. I might not have suffered so greatly over the years. I remember being told, some 25 years down the track, that I was still in deep shock, that I had never really fully recovered or come to terms with my tremendous loss and grief. Even now, I have days when I feel I have never really moved on, never had the strength to build a new life. But then I have had nothing to build my life around.

In the days that followed the death of the girls I felt myself withdrawing from Brian. I was completely lost in my grief and trying desperately just to get through each day. When night-time finally came I would fall into an exhausted, albeit troubled, sleep. I knew that Brian was also grieving, yet I found his behaviour quite odd and more than slightly disturbing. Each night he would wait for me to come to bed and impose himself on me. Making love to him was the last thing I wanted to do and I tried to explain this to him and would even physically turn my back on him.

He would keep insisting we have sex; he would not give up his insistence. I spoke to a friend, Wilma Evans, about this and she said, "June, in today's world this is considered rape. Even in marriage!"

Each time he approached me I would struggle with him

until finally I was too tired to fight him any longer and gave in to his manly strength.

I know now that he was just trying to hold on to me, that he felt that if he could make me pregnant then he would not lose me. However, at the time I was repulsed by his behaviour and his actions only served to push me further away from him.

Brian was aware when I married him that I was desperate for more children. It was three years before he admitted he would never have a child with me.

I was just so angry I packed a bag and went to stay with my friend Gwen Martin. After a couple of days Stephen and Cathy came to me and said, "Mum, you must come home, Brian is in a state. His blood pressure is up." I went back home and said to him, "Well, Brian, I'm back, but the next time I go I will never return to you." I was very bitter because I had been so desperate for more children for so many years.

Despite the nightly ritual we were now engaging in, I could see that Brian was trying to be supportive. He took care of most of the funeral arrangements for me. I only had one request. I wanted white coffins. To me the girls were so young, so pure and perfect, anything but white coffins was totally unacceptable.

Angela and Lyndy went through school and college together. Both worked in banking in the city of Sydney. At one stage the three girls were going to have the one Requiem Mass but for some reason these plans were changed. Angela's brother, Peter, belonged to a religious order. Angela had been sitting with the girls that fateful morning.

Peter Larkin had hymns printed especially for the services. I don't recall if Angela's Mass was held immediately before or after the girls. It was all a blur.

Early on the morning of the funeral I remember fussing. What would I wear? It was extremely important to me to wear something the girls liked. In fact, throughout the whole day of the funeral the thought that the girls were in those white coffins never occurred to me. I had no thought of their bodies lying in their coffins and I never thought to look inside to see them one last time. I did not shed a tear that day. No-one seemed to think my behaviour odd; however, it seems terribly odd to me now. “What the hell did it matter what I wore! My two darlings were in their coffins, they would not know!” Maybe this was my way of putting off making the final break with them. I was going through the motions of attending a funeral. Yet not once did I contemplate that it was my girls dead in those white coffins.

The funeral was held at Saint Patrick’s Church at Parramatta and the church was packed with people. There seemed to be hundreds of people. I was fearful the press would be at the church. This would have been just awful. It was such a private time for us all. To my sheer relief there was no press and I was extremely thankful for this. When I left the church my dear friend Len Edmondson was standing at the door. I had not seen him for some years. We did not speak. We just squeezed hands.

* * *

I was about 26 years old when I first met Len. Somehow I was the first secretary on the steering committee of the original Parents without Partners (PWP) organisation in New South Wales. PWP was formed for men and women rearing children alone or having access to their children. We had wonderful weekend picnics at the Lane Cove National Park. Barry Gilcrist ran around all day with this dead chook raffle to raise money for us. I never wanted to win that raffle – the chook wasn’t the best by the end of the day. We also had street stalls to raise money for Xmas parties and house parties on a Saturday night. Len never had any children. He had been married to a lady with children. He always stood out because he was much older than the rest of us. He had a lovely head of snow-white hair and I saw him as an English gentleman. He was keeping company with one of our ladies. I did not know him very well. He drove a Volvo and on the weekend he rode a motorbike in those days. I heard on our grapevine that he would not be attending our outings for some weeks as he had had an accident and broken his leg. Also, his lady friend had dropped him. This seemed awful to me. He lived at Coogee. I went to his home one Saturday afternoon, knocked on his door and offered to chauffeur him to that day's outing.

So began a 20-year friendship. We had a, perhaps, strange relationship. We were affectionate to each other, but it never developed into a physical relationship. I loved motorbikes. We went all over NSW on his bike. I guess we loved each other deeply. We always went dutch.

Towards the end of the year when the girls died he phoned me to say he was going to Adelaide for a couple of weeks. I was not able to leave Sydney at that time. He motored to Adelaide and I flew down to meet him a week later. I had my first look at Adelaide and we travelled home via the coast road. So began my love affair with Victoria, the Great Ocean Road and the beautiful Victorian coast. I have always said I knew when I have crossed the border because it is always so green. We travelled to Coonabarabran and there I was forced to climb my first and only mountain. Mountain climbing is not my scene.

Shortly after we met he built a lovely two-storey home at Cross Street, Castle Hill for his mother and himself. We used to take the girls bushwalking near his home. He lived there until he died.

I moved to Perth and not long after he phoned me. He was off to England again and would I like to meet him over there. I found a lady to look after my business in Perth and I set off for the United Kingdom.

We were having a great time. It was in Germany that he asked me to marry him. I went into shock mode; nothing could have been further from my mind. My rejection not only spoilt the remainder of our holiday, it injured out long-standing friendship. I felt so sad. Len was a man who loved women and women's company. He dearly wished for a successful marriage. (later)

* * *

Father Frank Williams came down to Sydney from Wyong on the Central Coast to conduct the Requiem Mass in Saint Patrick's Church at Parramatta where the three girls attended school, made their first communion and went on to be confirmed. Frank had been a wonderful support to me over all the years when Cathy was so ill with the brain tumour. I wanted Cathy and Lyndy to have the best resting place available, so I decided to buy a large plot to accommodate the girls, and large enough for Stephen and myself when our time came to be buried. I chose a beautiful Rose Garden at Pinegrove Memorial Park and I asked Stephen if he wanted some input into the arrangements I was making for the girls burial. "June," he said, "I would like you to place a large granite headstone on top of the girls'. I never want Cath to be disturbed." I made sure his wishes were carried out.

There was opposition from Brian about the cost of the plot where the girls were to be buried. He felt it was too expensive, but he did not deter me. I sold my car to pay for the plot of ground on a hill in the Rose Garden at Pinegrove. It was a beautiful plot in a lovely, peaceful place with perpetual care.

Cathy and Lyndy deserved the best and they had it.

My girls were buried at Pinegrove on 24th January, 1977. It was Cathy and Stephen's first wedding anniversary.

We were outside the church and I remember turning to Stephen and saying, "Stephen, it's your first wedding anniversary today. Cathy intended to cut the top layer of her wedding cake. Will we still cut it?" I was in complete denial. Stephen just shook his head and dropped his eyes.

That night after the funeral, my Aunt Ella stayed with me as she did not want me to be alone and she sensed there was growing tension between Brian and myself. She came over and put a comforting arm around me and said, "Make yourself comfortable, love. Take off your shoes and loosen the belt on your skirt." She proceeded to undo my belt and my skirt dropped about my ankles. I had lost a lot of weight in that week.

The house had been full of visitors for a week. Then there was no-one. Human nature is like that, I guess. People like to be in on the drama of life. Afterwards they get on with their lives and you are left to get on with yours. And that is when the impact of the insurmountable loss really came into focus.

My life became a nightmare – a daymare – to totally crush my spirit my body – my soul and my heart.

They say life begins at 40.

My life ended at 40. Forty and four months to the day.

My life ended, but I was still breathing, still existing.

And even though there have been times I have wished it otherwise, I have gone on breathing and existing.

CHAPTER 16

THE AFTERMATH

A week after the girls' funeral I was admitted to hospital for a blood transfusion. The shock of the girls' death had caused an ulcer to burst in my stomach and I was so weak I could hardly function. The doctor on duty informed me that my haemoglobin was so low that I could have had heart failure. Brian had come with me to the hospital and was sitting quietly, listening to what the doctor was saying. I was lying in the hospital bed with a drip in my arm and he was sitting beside my bed. Finally, he stood up and announced that he was going home. For some reason I had expected him to stay overnight. I needed him to stay longer, I did not want to be alone. I pleaded with him. "Please stay the night with me, I'm so afraid!" But he simply nodded his head, turned away and left me there alone. I have never forgotten that night and the feeling of desperate aloneness I felt. The dark emptiness of the room closed in around me. The sterile smell of the hospital ward engulfed me. Terror gripped me and I lay in the strange, uncomfortable hospital bed unable to move. Yet, I felt like I was falling, sinking into a dark and bottomless pit and no-one was there to save me. I held that against Brian for a long time.

Some days later the doctor declared me fit enough to go home and I was discharged from the hospital. Brian came to collect me. The drive from Sydney to Doonside where we lived took about an hour and the whole way home I felt like I was in some kind of void. I had withdrawn from Brian.

I knew this, I was conscious of it, but I felt there was nothing I could do about it. I didn't know what to say to him, it was like we were two strangers rather than husband and wife. When I walked in the door of the home that Brian and I shared in Doonside I was filled with emptiness. I felt the only emotion left in my marriage was grief. My grief for the loss of my girls and the grandchildren I would never have. Brian also grieved for everything he had lost, for I am sure that he had realised very early on that he had lost me forever. As part of my grieving process I held this terrible grudge against him. I felt that he had intentionally deprived me of another child. And the catalyst was he still had his son Steven, and he still had his chance for grandchildren. And yet he had deprived me of ever having any children or grandchildren. He had taken away my future. Yet life went on and I trudged along with it.

A few weeks after the death of the girls the phone rang one night and Brian answered it. I heard him say, "No you can't," then "No you can't speak to Lyndy, she's dead." I ran and grabbed the phone from him.

I was sobbing, "Can I help you?"

"Yes, I'm a friend of Lyndy's. Look, I don't know what's going on there. I had a date to meet Lyndy for lunch today. She has never let me down before. It's in my diary. We meet once a month. Could you please put her on the phone?" She was exasperated. My wounds were gashed opened all over again as I tried to tell her what had happened to our darling Lyndy.

She just kept saying over and over, "She has never let me down before. She has never let me down before. She is normally so reliable. We always meet once a month!"

She suddenly hung up on me. I never heard from her again, I didn't ever know her name. But then Lyndy had so many friends, I had never been able to keep track of them all.

I, on the other hand, was becoming more and more withdrawn as the weeks passed. I was looking for a reason to go on living, I was hanging on by only the barest of threads.

I was born on 18th September.

Lyndy was born on 18th September.

Lyndy was 18 years old when she died.

She died on 18th January.

18 weeks later there was an inquest into the girls' death.

The inquest into the Granville Train Disaster was to be held early in June 1977. I was determined to know more of what happened that fateful day – the day that had changed my life for ever. I went alone to the inquest. I feel sure there were friends who would have gone with me but I did not want anyone to deter me, so I told no-one I was going, or that I had been to the inquest. I drove myself to Sydney. I parked the car and walked up the steps of the Glebe Coroners' Court. I needed to hear what the coroner had to tell me. I remember praying that the press would not accost me and they didn't, that would have been too much for me to bear.

A police sergeant came and spoke to me and I told him why I was there and he stayed with me the whole day. There was another lady there also – she had lost her son in the Granville Train Disaster. The policeman told me, "You are fortunate, your girls died instantly. They barely had time to look up, they had not moved from their seats. I had to tell that other lady her son died of asphyxiation and she is devastated."

"I don't consider myself fortunate in any way!" I said to him bitterly. He put his arm around me and just shook his head!

The hearing was very graphic. I remember the magistrate speaking about an unidentified arm that had been found. He looked at me and said it did not belong to either of my girls.

I still remember having a photo of the girls with me that day, and walking up to people who were passengers on the train, and asking them if they remembered seeing Cathy or Lyndy on that day. I was desperate to know more about that day, more about why they were travelling on the fourth carriage, the carriage that carried so many fatalities. I found a man who recognised them.

"Yes," he nodded sadly, "I knew them by sight, they were always in my carriage. I always travelled in the second carriage, but no, I don't recall seeing them that morning."

Now Cathy, Lyndy and Angela always, and I mean always, travelled in the second carriage! I knew this for sure as I travelled with them often enough. I sewed for the girls in the bank and I often went to give them a fitting in their lunchroom before work. I knew the procedure – Lyndy and I would board the train at Doonside. When we got near to Parramatta Station, Lyn would go to the doorway and watch for Angie and Cathy standing on the platform. The big deal was to all sit together, all travel together. Of course it didn't always happen that way.

On the 18th January, Cathy, Lyndy and Angela were all sitting together, so they told me at the inquest. But they were in the fourth carriage… why were they not on the second carriage? They always travelled on the second carriage. This information left me stunned!

I became a mother on a mission!

I was obsessed with what happened on that fateful morning, the last day my girls were alive on this earth. The last day they would dress, run for the train and all meet and travel together to work in the city of Sydney.

I had to know why the girls were travelling in the fourth carriage that day, when they had always travelled in the second carriage.

There were no casualities on the second carriage, some were injured, but they all survived. There was not one fatality. Not one person died. Eight people died on the first carriage.

Forty-four people died on the third carriage and 31 people perished on the fourth carriage. My two darlings were among the 31 on that fourth carriage.

Around this time my marriage fell apart. I was filled with such bitterness. One day I just packed some of my things and moved back into my house in Parramatta. The same house that Stephen and Cathy had lived in after they were married. Stephen was still living there and he seemed happy to have the company.

One morning, a lady who lived across the road from me in Victoria Road, Parramatta, came over to speak to me.

She said, "I watched Cathy go off to work that morning. I seemed to just come indoors when the news of the train disaster came over the radio, and I said to my husband, dear God, that little girl could have been on that train!"

I honed in on her, asking her question after question. Could she tell me anything at all about that morning, if she had spoken to Cathy, was there anything she could remember?

"Well now," she said, "as a matter of fact her dog, Sambo, got out that morning and he was following her. I watched her bring Sambo back home and lock him in the back garden, and then she went running up the road, probably running late for her train by that time!"

I left her and went inside. I was shaking, my hands were shaking. I was crying, angry and distraught. I stewed over this all morning! In my own mind I reconstructed the whole thing. Sambo had got out. Sambo had made Cathy late for her train. And Lyndy would have been waiting for her, and she probably jumped off the train with Angie and the three of them re-boarded the train. On the fourth carriage!

The fourth carriage, in which every one of the 31 passengers was to die! My mission was accomplished. In my mind I finally convinced myself I knew what had happened that dreadful morning.

Sambo was to blame!

Sambo caused the girls to die.

Sambo caused all this dreadful devastation! I dwelt on it for hours.

Finally, I decided I had to kill Sambo. Yes, I would have to tie him up, then get the axe and kill him, chop him up. I tied Sambo to a post and went to the shed, but I could not find the axe. I searched everywhere, but I just could not find it. By the time Stephen came home I was crying and hysterical. Sambo was still tied to the post on the back patio. I told him everything that had happened that day. I could not stop sobbing. Stephen took Sambo away and I never saw him again.

I was out of my mind. I just went crazy, crazy with grief and anger. How could this hateful animal have caused her death? This dog she loved so dearly. Sambo should not be alive when he had directly caused the deaths of my two darling girls.

CHAPTER 17

ALL-CONSUMING GRIEF

Sometime early in 1977 I was informed I was to make a claim against the NSW Government Railways for the death of the girls. Although I was not living with Brian any more he had offered to come with me to Blacktown to see a solicitor and I had gratefully accepted. I remember standing in the street and my legs would not seem to work. I had to concentrate really hard, to tell myself to put one foot forward and then the other. It was the strangest sensation.

Eventually the claim went to court. Stephen and I attended the case and a settlement was made. I felt as if I had been swept along in the tide of it all. Nothing could ever compensate me for my terrible loss. Nothing made much sense any more and I felt that I was beginning to lose my composure. My head was spinning and I felt ill equipped to deal with all that was happening. By this time my GP had sold his practice and was working for the government insurance company. I realise now he was probably not much help, maybe even a hindrance to me.

Nevertheless, Stephen took me across the road to his office after the case was finished. When I saw my the doctor I remember him remarking to me, "Now, June, it's time to let it go, get on with your life." I just looked at him. I was completely drained, washed out. It had all been a harrowing experience.

The doctor gave me a Valium injection and by the time Stephen helped me into his car I was out to it, and did not wake until the next morning.

Two weeks after the girls died I had a phone call to say John's brother, Georgie, was dying with cancer and I went to their house in Clyde to see him. His wife, Jean, met me at the door and whispered "Georgie doesn't know about your girls. I don't think he could stand the shock, please be careful. "

In spite of my grief I somehow found the courage to sit by his bed and hold his hand. He chatted away to me and told me "Cathy and Lyndy came to the hospital to see me in their lunch hour one day. It was lovely to see them." I remember feeling proud that they had taken the time to visit their Uncle Georgie in hospital.

When I was leaving Jean told me there had been a terrible mix-up. The whole family thought for some days that it was their daughters Julieanne and Carolyn, who had been killed. I sat in my car crying for a long time. I felt resentful.

Some time later I was shopping at Quakers Hill, browsing through a carpet warehouse, when I overheard a woman; she was just a voice behind some rolls of carpet. She was speaking in a happy, animated voice. They were discussing the Granville Train Disaster. This was something that happened to me quite often in those early days. It seemed that no matter where I went someone was talking about it. There was always someone to relate to me how they had just missed the train or that someone they knew was travelling on the train. It was like everyone wanted to be in on the drama.

I stood frozen to the spot. I had to hear once more another person's tale about the Disaster. I overheard this voice relating to the other voice "Oh yes, we were so lucky! We thought our daughter was a casualty in the Disaster. I knew she was on that train and when she didn't come home from work and had not phoned I was frantic. I rang the police, gave her details and reported her missing. Thankfully she finally came through the door the next day."

I dropped my bag and ran around the aisle to where she was standing chatting away happily to her friend. I grabbed her arm and said, "Oh excuse me, I overheard you talking about your daughter being on the train. Could I please ask you a question?"

"Are you okay?" she said. "You look quite ill!"

"Yes," I said. "I just need to know, does your daughter carry a large scar across the top of her head?" I thought immediately if this girl had a scar identical to Cathy's, she might be the cause of my question, "Why did it take so long to identify Cathy? Was she mistaken for Cathy?"

She looked at me quizzically, "Well yes, she had a brain tumour some years ago. I did report that to the police at the time."

"Oh," I said "and did you report it to the police when she arrived home safe?"

"Well no, when she came through the door I did not think it necessary. Are you sure you are okay?"

I moved away almost staggering. I had to get to the bottom of this. It was all too much of a coincidence. Here was a young woman, she lived in the next suburb, with an identical scar across the top of her head the same as Cathy had and for the same reason. They both had had a brain tumour operation some years before!

When I returned to my car I realised I did not have my handbag. I ran back inside and found it still on the floor where I had dropped it.

This was another dreadful setback. I now had something else to dwell on.

I'm not sure why but I hated that woman, the mother of that young girl. I didn't even know her name. She had a daughter home with her safe and sound and my girls were both in their graves. It all seemed so unfair.

* * *

It was a balmy, summer Sydney day and I had a call from a friend, Gwen Martin. On an impulse she rang and asked me to go with her and her son, Bradley, for a picnic on the banks of the Nepean River. We packed a picnic lunch between us and Gwen picked me up. We set off up the Great Western Highway to Penrith.

We ate our picnic lunch and shared a thermos of coffee. The day progressed pleasantly and Bradley was always such a delight to be with. We laughed a lot, as Brad was such a happy young boy. As we sat there chatting I felt particularly calm and at peace. We were chatting about mundane things, enjoying each other's company. We had been friends for over 10 years. Gwen and I met when our children were in the same ward at Children's Hospital.

I looked into the distance where there was a bridge crossing the Nepean River. A train was crossing the bridge as I looked up. I was thinking that it would be a Blue Mountains locomotive travelling to Katoomba.

Suddenly Gwen turned to me and said, "Gee, wouldn't it be exciting to see the train crash into the river!"

I sat staring at her. I was completely immobilised. I could not speak. I could not move.

She must have read my face as she quickly apologised. "Oh God, I'm sorry, Junee," she said.

I sat there thinking to myself, "Nobody, not even a close friend, has any idea of what I am going through or the thoughts that stay with me every waking moment of my days."

That moment, just those few cruel, thoughtless words, brought home to me how alone I was with my ever-engulfing grief.

That was the end of our tranquil afternoon.

A short time later I was shopping in Parramatta when I ran into a lady I had known some years before.

I immediately felt anxious as I asked, “Hello, how are you?”

The first thing she said was “Hi, how are the girls?” with a smile on her face.

Every part of my body went perfectly still. I just stood there looking into her eyes, unable to open my mouth, unable to move. I just stood there staring at her. Eventually she just walked away. I often wondered what she thought had happened to me, this happy-go-lucky young woman she had once known. This happy-go-lucky woman I used to be.

Another day while out shopping I ran into a lady I knew who had a son about the same age as Cathy. She had read in the paper about the death of Lyndy and offered me her sympathy. Then she smiled and said, “Oh well, at least you still have Cathy.” I just looked at her for what seemed like at interminable period of time, my throat closed up and I just couldn’t utter a sound. After a while I just walked away. Cathy had married and changed her name since I first met her. My wounds were laid open again and I no longer cared about anything or anyone.

I walked everywhere in those days seeing nothing.

I developed an awful fear of people. Grief is a most debilitating emotion! You go to bed with it. You wake up with it.

It has stayed with me all of my life.

I would walk the streets with my head down and often pop into a shop to avoid someone I knew.

* * *

I started seeing a psychiatrist, Dr Ian Martin, three times a week. Doctor Ian was not the usual run of the mill type psychiatrist. He specialised in treating people mainly from overseas, who had lost their whole families in war-torn parts of the world.

He talked to me, and he worked with me. I had much respect for him. He was a kind and compassionate man.

Lyndy and my birthdays were coming up on 18th September, and Ian had said, "June, be sure to start that day right. You must write a list of all the things to do that day and you must keep busy!"

I started that day with the best of intentions; I worked hard physically all morning in the garden. Then after lunch I decided to have a hot bath as I was aching all over from my morning in the garden. Then I decided I would go to the cemetery to visit the girls' grave. I was spending a great deal of my time up at Pinegrove with them those days.

I went in to run the bath, stood there looking at it and thought, "Gee, this bath is grotty, I should give it a good clean first!"

There was a mess caught in the plughole, and when I pulled it out I realised it was long hair. It had to be Cathy's hair! I clutched it to my heart with trembling hands. I tenderly shampooed it and dried it with the hair dryer. Here in my grasp was a handful of Cathy's beautiful long, blonde hair.

I had in my hands a part of her, a part of her body, her hair. I had something that belonged to my darling Cathy. I did not know what to do with it. I was in shock. Here in my hands was a mass of Cathy's hair. A part of her!

"Oh my God, what will I do with it? Should I run outside and burn it?" I sobbed.

I did that, I burnt her lovely hair, and then almost immediately I regretted doing it. Sometime later in the day my friends, Lynne and Fred Bastian, rang me to wish me a happy birthday. I remember sobbing into the phone, trying to tell them what had happened. But they could not understand, they simply could not comprehend my pain.

The death of a child is a grief, a sadness, like no other. It is a silent, isolating grief. The silence comes from friends and acquaintances. When you attempt to speak of a dead child there is always this awful wall of embarrassed silence. In time you cease to speak about them, as their silence is unbearable. None of my friends would ever intentionally hurt me, but in their ignorance they did.

Those were terrible days of despair and desolation.

Unfortunately that embarrassed silence still exists today. Over 30 years later when I attempt to talk about my darling daughters to my friends they are embarrassed; they don't know what to say. In time you cease to speak about them.

* * *

I was visiting my friend Betty Mitchell one day. She was reading the newspaper and she said, "There has been another train derailment" I turned to her and said, "I hope they're all dead." Betty was shocked by my statement and replied, "Oh, June surely you don't mean that."

I had shocked myself also.

I had a session with my psychiatrist a few days later. I asked him why I had reacted in that way, why I had felt that way.

Doctor Ian in his usual quiet, patient way explained my reaction to me.

"June, your subconscious is crying out for someone who will maybe understand how you are feeling. The emotions you are experiencing, you are not wishing this on someone else out of meanness," he said.

The death of your only children is as if your body, mind and spirit have been smashed against a brick wall. It falls to the ground in a million pieces… The years slip by. You slowly glue all the pieces together. Your heart, your body, your spirit, your emotions, you slowly attempt to make whole again. Like a broken piece of porcelain the pieces can never really be whole or stable. They crumble so easily.

A simple thing will make the glue come apart. You have to pick yourself up and so you are trying to glue your life together once more.

Year after year after year after year.

In October 1977 Lynne and Fred Bastian encouraged me to go to the German Festival with them and a group of their friends. The Bastians had been my long-standing friends and their home was my safe haven in those days. It was the place I could go to, a place where I felt safe and could just walk in any time. There was never an issue with them. They accepted me and came close to understanding what I was going through.

I will hold them in my heart for ever.

It was at the German Festival that I first met Helen Dalrymple. Helen is a unique, wonderful person. At times I believe she saved my life. On that night at the Festival she became my friend.

Even though Helen had never known my girls, she kept turning up at my home, day after day, to support me. There were times she would come and I could not so much as make her a cup of tea. I spent my days sitting in a chair staring into space or walking. I would walk for miles, with my head down. Seeing no-one or nothing.

Helen was wonderful. Eventually she encouraged me to play carpet bowls. I was never much of a player. However, I did start to go out even though I could not talk to the other bowlers or communicate with anyone.

I was at least getting out of the house. It was a start.

That Octoberfest was the beginning of a wonderful, long-standing friendship.

Over the years I moved around from State to State. I have never been able to settle, but I have never lost contact with Helen Dalrymple.

CHAPTER 18

THE MIRROR CRACKS

As each month slipped by another tiny fragment of my mind slipped away with it. Not that this is what I would have said at the time. If anyone was to ask me about my state of mind at the time I would have told them that I was okay, I was dealing with my loss and trying to move on, because that's what we're taught to say from a very early age. When people ask us how we are we're supposed to say, "Fine, thank you, how are you?" People don't want to hear that things are not going so well, that you're about to lose the plot, they just want to hear that you're fine so they can get on with their lives. The truth of the matter was that I was not fine, not fine at all. My world, which was once filled with laughter and hope, had now become an empty void and the silent, isolating loneliness was deafening. I tried to keep myself going. I would try to set myself small tasks to do each day so that I would feel like I had accomplished something with my day. Each morning I would get up, have a shower, get dressed and make myself a pot of coffee. Then I would clean the house from top to bottom. It seemed very important that the house be kept in order. I would vacuum and dust and polish until the surfaces gleamed. Only then did I feel comfortable that I had done enough. This done I would change my clothes and drive to Granville, park my car in a little street adjacent to the railway line and walk the tracks east and west of the tragic scene of the Granville Train Disaster where my two daughters had lost their lives on 18th January of that year.

There were still burnt-out fragments of victims' lives scattered along the tracks and railway sleepers in the area.

I found solace in walking the tracks, as though I was somehow a little bit closer to my girls. Their lives had come to an abrupt end and the suddenness and finality of it all was something I could not deal with. I wanted to see them, I wanted to be with them, but they were just not there. I was searching for fragments of their lives, something I could hang on to. As I walked the tracks and sifted through the rubble images of the girls would flash through my mind. Lyndy and Cathy as little girls running home from the shops through Prince Alfred Park laughing with mischief. I would recall Cathy as a bride, so young and beautiful, with her whole life ahead of her. Lyndy, cheeky and outspoken as she was, sitting at the table eating mulberry pie while on holiday at Salamander Bay.

I walked those tracks as if I was in a kind of fantasy world that I had created especially for myself. This was a place that belonged to my girls and me alone. A place filled with my memories of them. It was a place I chose to go more and more, and once there I would try and stay as long as I could. It was the one place I could go where I felt closer to my girls. But all too soon the sounds of life going on around me would interrupt and drag me back to reality. I would hear the honk of a car horn or the sound of a crane on a nearby building site.

The pain was almost unbearable.

One day, after many months of walking the tracks, I finally found something that belonged to one of my girls, a fragment of their lives. I couldn't believe my eyes. I knew immediately that it was the gold watchband belonging to my Lyndy's Seiko watch.

I bent down and picked it up and clasped it tightly in my hand. I held on to that watchband like I was holding on to Lyndy. My Lyndy, my special child. God I loved her and I wanted her back. I wanted her back. The tears streamed down my face without restraint and I didn't care. The anger, the bitterness, the never-ending, aching loneliness, it all came out and I just crouched there on the old, worn-out tracks clutching the dirty and scratched watchband, sobbing. I had finally found what I had been looking for.

The devastating heartache and anger I felt as I stood up by the side of the railway track holding this piece of my darling, special child in my hand was crushing. This watch was a gift that had been so important to her. Stephen had bought Cathy a Seiko for Christmas. Lyndy and Cathy had always received the same or similar gifts right throughout their lives, and seeing the look of complete and utter joy on Lyndy's face when she opened the box had made the watch worth every cent I had paid for it. And now I held the watchband in my hand. I had the watch, but not the special girl it had been bought for. Life was too cruel.

I had another link in the broken chain that was my heart, our lives.

I trudged along the uneven ground with the watchband firmly in my hand to where I could scamper up the incline at the side of the tracks and through the hole in the fence, back to my car parked in a nearby street. Once in the car, I carefully placed the watchband in the middle console of the car and drove home. When I arrived home I carefully cleaned the watchband and placed it in my jewellery box next to the watch face. I was home once again with yet another fragment of my Lyndy.

That night when I turned out the light and crawled into

bed I did not cry as I expected I would. It was as though I had cried away all my tears and there were none left to shed. After months of struggling to come to terms with the death of my girls I was no further along the path to understanding. My life just didn't make sense and I couldn't see how it ever would again. I had lost too much. The struggle to survive; to just get through each day, was too exhausting. I longed for sleep, for never-ending sleep, for in sleep there is no pain, there are dreams and nightmares, but no pain.

I stared into the night sky for a long time, and as I lay there staring at the stars the idea came to me as if it had been there all along, but was just waiting for me to acknowledge it and give it form. The longer I lay there, the more sense it all made. It was the answer to everything and there was no other alternative. I started to feel a bubble of excitement from somewhere deep inside me.

I would do it on 18th January, exactly one year after the death of the girls. My breathing became more rapid as I concentrated hard. How would I do it? I lay there thinking. The 6.05 Commuter Train from the Blue Mountains. Yes, that was perfect. I would stand on the new Bold Street Bridge and wait for the 6.05 Commuter Train from the Blue Mountains, the same one that had caused the death of my girls, and I would throw myself off the bridge in front of the train. Yes, that's what I would do. My excitement was growing, I would be with my girls, finally I would be with my girls and we would all be together. I lay there that night for a very long time just staring at those stars in the sky as if they had given me the answer to my prayers. I had my plan; it was mine and mine alone. I felt a great excitement. I was conspiring a grand plan that no-one but I must know about. I would need to plan it with precision and take care to keep it my secret. As I fell asleep that night I felt more at peace than I had since the day of the disaster. Here at last was the answer that I had been looking for.

I continued to visit Ian Martin, my psychiatrist, three times a week, and when I wasn't with the doctor I was visiting my girls' graves at Pinegrove.

I very much liked and respected Ian. I would talk to him for a good three hours every week and he felt that I was making progress. But he did not know about my plan. I had guarded my secret with my life, and each time I left Doctor Ian's office I felt a bit smug that I had come through another session without giving away my secret. It felt good, it kept me going, it gave me purpose. I felt lighter and there was a spring in my step that hadn't been there before.

In retrospect I can now see that my plan was dark and sinister. But I did not see it that way at the time. In those days it was the gossamer thread that held my life together. No other plan gave me more purpose. It was something to think about, a purpose to function from day to day. It was a purpose to bathe, walk, sleep, eat and clean. Even cook an evening meal for Stephen and myself.

The date for the inquest into the Granville Train Disaster was fast approaching, and was scheduled to take place very soon after my 41st birthday and Lyndy's 19th birthday. I looked ahead to the date of the inquest and our birthdays with trepidation and wondered how I would make it through these very significant and painful events. But I underestimated the power of my secret plan, and in the days preceding both the inquest and our birthdays I found myself focusing much of my attention on the final details of my plan. I would sit for hours, making a mental list of all the things I needed to finalise before my last day. It was as if I was planning to go on holiday and my escape from the harsh reality that was my world was in anticipating my trip.

I got through the inquest and I also somehow survived our birthdays. This was the first time in 19 years we had not been together on our birthday. My secret plan was my twisted pole of strength that helped me through those two events. I longed for the day that I would execute my plan.

Approximately one week before the first anniversary of the Granville Train Disaster I was spring-cleaning the house, having a big clean up, throw out. I got to the mantelpiece above the fireplace in the dining room. This was the place where Stephen and I kept letters to be posted, bills to be paid. I picked up a folded piece of paper and opened it up. It was just another thing wanting attention I thought. I flipped open the letter with disinterest and the words leapt off the page and hit me like a slap in the face. The letter was written by a doctor and read "A patient of this doctor is in a frame of mind to commit suicide." I just kept reading this phrase over and over. "In a frame of mind to commit suicide. In a frame of mind to commit suicide." I stood there reading and rereading that letter. Realisation struck and I was jolted into sanity, reality. It was a mentally painful and frightening time. The gossamer thread had snapped.

Suddenly my plan had a name… Suicide.

I immediately changed my clothes, grabbed my keys and locked the door. I walked up Victoria Road and along Philip Street, Parramatta as if in a fog. Then I was in Doctor Ian Martin's surgery. The remainder of that day is just a blank. All I recall is Ian taking me in his car to Northmead Private Hospital.

I was in hospital for about 10 days to two weeks. Much of that period of time I was under heavy sedation, but I do recall stipulating that I would never have shock treatment. It was never on my agenda and I was very upfront about that. I had seen what shock treatment had done to my girls' father. I also refused to go to group therapy. How could I bear my soul to a lot of strangers?

On 18th January, 1978 I was heavily sedated, unable to move my body, legs or arms at all. I kept watching the clock on the wall. 7am, 7.15am, 7.30am, 7.45am, the minutes ticked by. I was struggling, struggling, trying to get out of bed. I just had to get out of that bed and carry out my plan. Today was the day, it was the day I had planned so carefully and for so long. I had to get out of bed. The minutes were slipping by. My plan was in danger of being destroyed, taken away from me for ever. This could not happen, not now when I was so close. The minutes slipped by and I still couldn't move. 8.05am, 8.10am, 8.15am. My chance for peace. My chance to be with my darlings, my Cathy and my Lyndy, had slipped away for ever.

My months of planning, my intention to throw myself off the Bold Street Bridge at Granville in front of the 6.05am from Katoomba on 18th January, 1978 had been taken away from me for ever. Desolation and despair were again my constant companions. I was back with that painful state of sanity. I could not take it, NO, I would not make it. I had to be with my girls.

CHAPTER 19

ADOPTION

It was shortly after the death of my girls. Brian and I had separated and I had had a spell in a psychiatric ward of Concord Repat Hospital. Due to the fact that my body could not tolerate anti-depressant medication Doctor Ian was searching for an alternative.

He was desperately looking for some way to help me, looking for something to give me a reason to go on living. Trying to put something back into my life…

He was desperate to give me a reason to go on living!

He suggested artificial insemination.

Back in the 1970's 41 was considered too old to safely bear a normal child. The risks were thought to be too great. If I had a miscarriage or one of the many abnormalities possible with mature-age conception, I could be pushed over the edge.

In those days I often felt I was walking on the edge of a cliff, teetering backwards and forwards. Somehow I never quite fell over the cliff.

I was so close. Oh so often…

One day I was having a session with Doctor Ian and he offered me another alternative.

I could book into a major hospital in Sydney, spend one day there and come home with a new-born baby registered in my name.

I would never be given any information about the child. Not ever. I would be registered as the birth mother of this child. My name would be on the birth certificate. The child would be mine.

There was a sum of money involved.

I found myself with a lot to think about. This was something I had to go over carefully. It was something that would affect me for the rest of my life.

I was in turmoil for days. Could I embark on this wonderful, frightening journey? I moved from wonderful highs to terrible lows!

Excitement turned to fear and back to excitement. I could feel this tiny baby boy in my arms.

Yes… the tiny baby boy had been born a week earlier! He was a breathing, living, little baby boy.

I approached Brian and even though we were no longer living together, he agreed to give me the $1000 required, if I decided to go ahead and have this tiny baby boy in my life. ($1000 was a lot of money in those days.)

I would have a child of my own again.

My next step was to visit my GP Doctor Christie, to have his opinion on what I should do. My emotions were torn in so many different directions at that time.

Doctor Christie was horrified! He said, "This child will be an IT! Who will you say its father is? What will you tell people? This is against the teachings of the Catholic Church." He threw all the negatives at me. All the things I had given no thought to.

Doctor Christie was so against this whole venture, I lost my confidence.

I returned to Doctor Ian and told him I had decided against having the baby in my life.

He was very understanding. I understood and appreciated that he was acting out of desperation to help me. He wanted to save me. He was so desperate to help me.

So many times over the years I have thought about that baby boy!

Often I have thought of him with much regret at my decision all those years ago.

He would now be a man of 30-odd years of age and possibly have children of his own.

I don't go there very often.

Dr Ian was a wonderful, compassionate man. I was fortunate to have him in my life at that time.

CHAPTER 20

RUNNING WITH DEMONS

I had been battling along for a couple of years, struggling to exist from one day to the next, and I was still seeing Doctor Ian when a friend encouraged me to go to a club for the evening. As time went on I was finding it harder to communicate or even talk to people, however, I went to the club with her. Audrey was a good dancer and spent most of the night waltzing around the floor. As I sat watching the dancers, a woman whom I had never seen before approached me and I soon realised by her manner that she obviously knew who I was.

This stranger, this woman I had never seen before, touched my hand and said, "Don't watch the television tomorrow night, whatever you do, don't watch TV tomorrow night!" Of course I could not resist checking to see what was screening on TV that Sunday night. I knew in my heart it would be something relating to the Granville Disaster!

This Fabulous Century! "The Granville Train Disaster" was screening.

And of course I watched it. I was devastated. It was so

graphic. This was just another setback and I was in a mess all over again.

Ever since the death of the girls, I continually came across these drama seekers, usually women, who in some warped way wanted to make a celebrity out of me! My life was certainly no celebration.

I have come to the realisation that going out to the club that night was to directly lead to a dramatic change in the direction of my whole future, and I have never been able to decide if the direction I chose was to my good or to my detriment.

However, I had a lot of thinking to do. I had a friend who had moved to Perth the previous year and I decided to pay her a visit to escape Sydney for a while.

I stayed with her for a couple of weeks and we discussed me going to Perth to live.

"Let's have a look around at some real estate," suggested Betty. I found a lovely house in Hamersley, a beach suburb, and the next suburb over from where Betty and her daughter, Vicki, lived. I decided to go back to Sydney and think things through, and then maybe make the move to Perth on a permanent basis.

Within 6 weeks I had moved, installed myself in my beautiful, new home at 3 Eglington Crescent, Hamersley, Perth.

Me on my way to Perth...What a drive!!!

CHAPTER 21

A LIFE OF SILENCE

So began one of the loneliest, most goddamn awful periods in my life. I was in a strange State, I knew but one family, I was at a time in my life where everything was new, I had lost my ability to mix and make friends, I had lost all my confidence, my self-esteem, and my grief was overwhelming!

I found the only way I could get from day to day was to make lists, lists of how to get through each day, lists of things I could say to people, lists for everything.

Every night I would make a list for the following day.

- 7am get out of bed.
- 7:05am have a shower.
- 7.30 breakfast.
- 8am clean the pool, etc.

In the early days of living in Perth I worked with disadvantaged children and their parents. I found that when I was out of the house meeting people and helping people I usually managed to put my sadness behind me. The problem was I always had to come home to an empty house. The loneliness was something I could not escape. There were times at night when I would drink a half glass of brandy straight. I had never been a drinker and I found it hard to get the brandy down. However, I knew it would help to dull my senses and help me to just cry. I would then sob my heart out.

Then I would give in to my anger. I was so, so angry in those days. I was angry with the government. Angry with my friends because they had children and I didn't. I was angry at the whole damn world. Yes, the brandy helped me express my anger. I would then begin to smash things, anything, on the kitchen floor.

I lived in a dark, lonely hole of grief.

My life, my mind, my body, my psyche and my emotions were all smashed up.

Why was everything precious taken away from me, destroyed?

For years I was confused. I could not focus. I could not function properly. Where was I going? What did the future hold for me? Did I have a future?

I just pushed along from day to day… 30 years on I still get these traumatic, confusing days… I am amazed that I have existed all these years… To the outside world my life is that of a normal person… To my inside private world my life will never be exactly normal again… As I get older it just gets harder.

Over time I have smashed crockery, crystal and vases. Anything I could find that was breakable. The next morning I would wonder what had ever come over me. I then had all this mess to clean up again.

After a time Stephen, Cathy's husband, came to stay with me in Perth and the crockery smashing came to an abrupt end. I am not sure if it was due to having some company in the house or maybe I though I could not vent my anger when Stephen was there in the house with me.

Those early days in Perth were traumatic and lonely. I sometimes wonder how I ever got through them. Looking back now I can never make sense of my going to Perth to live. It was just a crazy thing to do.

CHAPTER 22

STEPPING INTO THE WORLD OF HIGH FASHION RETAIL

Eventually, through the Mitchells, I made a few friends.Betty's son, Ian, was good to me. We are still friends today. He stays in touch with me still. Ian took me to meet his accountant, Serge, who became my accountant and friend; he still is to this day. I talked to him about things I could do, to get my life back on to some sort of track.

Serge questioned me about what I had done in my life. I told him everything. My first job was in the fabric shop, Coco Pedy's, in Granville. Then I did office work, running a small corner store with my mum, as an upstairs cook in a hotel, working nights in a milk bar on Central Station in Sydney, working in an all night café, 14 years teaching driving and back to office work. Finally I had studied for 4 years for a diploma to be a fashion teacher immediately before losing the girls.

"With your fashion training, why not look at buying a fashion boutique?" he said.

I had very limited experience in retail, just a few unsuccessful weeks when I was 15 years old, so I did not feel very confident.

"Serge, I will give it some thought," I said.

I could never have known that the seed of thought Serge planted that day would bloom into such a powerful plant.

I was on the road to many, many years as a very successful businesswoman in the world of retail; high-fashion retail.

My accountant's simple statement would eventually set me up to be very comfortably off in my senior years. With some serious financial ups and downs in between!

The first business for sale that I investigated was Champagne Bubble Boutique, in Centreways Arcade, the old Zimples Arcade. This was the one; I knew this was the right place for me to begin my new venture. This was the business I wanted.

After several weeks of unsuccessful negotiations due to the reason they were asking too much for the goodwill, I enlisted the help of my accountant.

We went to speak to the owners and I wasn't getting anywhere with them. I vividly remember how my accountant literally pushed me out the door and said, "June, go for a walk!" After some considerable time, he emerged from the Champagne Bubble Boutique. He had a signed contract in his hand. They had agreed to my price.

"June, you are the proud owner of a business in the heart of Perth!" he told me.

This was no thanks to me, and my inability to suffer fools.

For the grand sum of $4000 I was a Perth businesswoman. I had a purpose, and what a purpose it was.

I really didn't know a thing about retail, and for the first couple of days I thought "All I have to do is stand behind the counter, collect the money, put the purchases in a bag and see the ladies out the door." What a shock I was in for!

Well, I proved to be a fast learner, and as the years went by I was considered to be one of the best buyers in the business. Buying this business opened up a whole new world to me.

I found myself in a world of shoplifters, a world of high

fashion, the gay community and prostitutes. I adopted an attitude of "if people had money to spend they were welcome in my store."

I learnt to buy into whatever market demands were in that particular season. On the subject of shoplifters, a problem I was unaware existed before buying the business, I quickly found that I had my share and I even caught a few!

One of them was a very good customer until she stole an expensive imported knit top and then came back wanting to purchase the matching skirt. I told her I would burn it before I would sell it to her! I passed her one day in the car park and she was wearing my knit top. She looked me right in the eyes with a smirk on her face. That moment was the beginning for me of a lifetime crusade against shoplifters. I was only operating a couple of weeks when these two, extremely well-dressed women came in, done up to the nines. They spent a lot of time browsing and finally made a lay-by of some garments. After they had left I discovered a silk blouse was missing. I was extremely upset and I called the police. They came promptly and while taking details asked me to describe these women. I told them they were very distinct, with long, dyed black hair, extremely thin and as I said to the detective there was something odd, but I could not put my finger on what it was. They asked me if I thought they could be transvestites. I had never heard the word before, however, I was learning quickly. It turned out these two were known to the police and they had been trying to get a lead on them for some time. Yes, they were transvestites and were both in the process of having a sex change. While the police were in the shop these women actually rang me to say they would be in the next day to collect their lay-by and would I be in the store, as they liked being served by me, as I was so nice. (They obviously knew I was new to the business of selling and they were coming to pick up some more freebies.)

I told them I would be there for them and asked what time

they would be in. At 9am the next morning the police were staked out in the coffee shop opposite, and when my customers arrived to pick up their lay-by they were there to arrest them. Life was certainly not dull in Champagne Bubble Boutique.

The detectives returned my silk blouse a few days later and said it would be some years before I saw them again.

I had discovered the world of shoplifting with all the dramas attached. As aware as I was I still lost things, but I was forever on the lookout. I no longer stood behind the counter, I was always out there on the floor.

I had some very good customers from the gay community, I found them easy to do business with as they had money to spend and I knew how to buy for them. I knew what they liked.

I learnt from my accountant how to balance my books. He was a wonderful friend and adviser over the years.

I knew I had to forever find new ways of acquiring and keeping customers and how to train staff, and I had some really great staff over the years and some I could have done without. One morning, after I had placed an ad in the newspaper for a salesperson, a 16 year-old-girl came laughing through the door, in answer to my ad. Her parents had told her words to the effect of "If you don't get a job and straighten yourself out we are finished with you." She had been everywhere. And at the age of 16 had done it all. She laughed all the time, but I never was sure how much of what she told me was true. However, I liked her as she made me feel good.

"I think I'll give her a try!" I thought. She tidied herself up and as she came from a retail family she learnt very quickly. She was honest and fairly reliable and she was with me for many years, and most of the time we had a really good relationship. I was always the boss and for that reason she respected me.

I had another young woman who worked for me part-time for a number of years. She was a lovely, honest girl, however, she never became a wonderful salesperson, but she was reliable and a real hard worker.

Occasionally she would have a drinking spree and come to work the next day in a foul mood. More than once she threatened to leave, then one day she came at this stunt and she got me on the wrong day.

I said ,"If you want to leave, well do it right now!" I don't know who got the biggest shock, her or me. I always regretted losing her, but business was business, however, I lost a good friend and employee.

My accountant had taken me under his wing and he always had some good advice for me. One of his many pieces of advice was, "June, you never eat, sleep or socialise with your staff." This is not always easy when you are very alone in a new city. I did often eat and socialise with my staff.

CHAPTER 23

GOOD FRIENDS

I made some really good friends in my years in the fashion business. They were all ladies in the same business as myself. I had made a decision soon after I arrived in Perth and realised how very lonely a new city can be. If anyone asked me to go somewhere or do something, I would. I would just say yes, and think about it later. Consequently, I was on the road to many years of overseas travel. I who had never held a passport in my life and I was in my early 40s.

Over the next 10 years, I travelled the world, or so it seemed to me. I had many trips to Bali, Singapore, Hong Kong, Bangkok, England, Ireland, Scotland and Wales, Spain, France, Switzerland, Germany, Italy, Hawaii, Canada and the U.S.A. Yet previous to moving to Perth I had never been any further than to drive up the coast from Sydney to Brisbane.

My travelling companions were mostly women, some of whom were customers I had met through my shop.

I had a lot of trips with my dear friend Norma. Norma owned a number of boutiques in Perth over the years and she was great to travel with. I remember we had travelled to Bangkok one time. It was late at night when we arrived at our hotel. We walked into our room and our bags were there waiting for us. I flopped on the bed exhausted. All I needed was a bath and a sleep. Norma walked in behind me and had a good look around, then she got mad, really mad, a thing I always thought she did wonderfully, and she said to me, "June this is not good enough, this room has not been cleaned properly." The bags had to go back out into the passageway, the management called and the room cleaned to Norma's satisfaction,

"They know we're here!" I thought. All I really wanted was a bath and a meal, which I got eventually, and the service was great after that, except for the bread rolls and butter. Now Norma had a thing about soft butter. If the butter was soft it always went back. Of all the people I travelled with over the years, I enjoyed Norma's company the most. She was just a sincere, true friend. She was great to hit the shops with, and we did just that. We shopped until we dropped.

A year or so after I went to Perth, my son-in-law Stephen came to stay for a while. His life was in tatters and he hadn't really worked since Cathy had died.

I thought of the time I walked into Cathy's bedroom and she was crying. "Whatever is wrong, darling?" I said. Cathy was always such a happy person.

She was crying because she had been thinking of Stephen. She said, "Mummy, I don't know what Stephen would ever do without me. I'm sure he could not live if I died." I was stuck for words for once. Neither one of us, Cathy nor I, could realise how soon Stephen would have to do just that; live without his Cathy.

Stephen was there with me for only a short time when he got a job, which he liked, and he made new friends. Stephen had always been introverted and understandably he became more so after his life fell apart. However, Stephen has always had the ability to make good friends and keep them. He went out often playing cards, snooker and all the things men like to do. We often had words as Stephen was very untidy and messy and I was a tidiness freak in those days.

I came home from work late one Thursday evening tired and irritable and he had obviously been out shopping. The empty shirt box was in the kitchen, there was rubbish in the bathroom, wrapping paper and sales dockets in his bedroom, and I thought "Just wait to he comes home!" Well, he strolled in the next morning about 10am. "Gee, love, I was worried about you, where have you been?" I said.

I was obviously over my tantrum, as he knew I would be.

"Oh," he said, "I knew I had left a mess, so I camped at the Mitchells'. I knew you would be okay this morning!"

While Stephen was with me I had a letter from my old friend in Sydney, Len. "June, I'm off overseas in March, why don't you come along?" he said. I didn't think too much about going or not going, as everything quickly fell into place for me. A friend who had just sold her business in the arcade where I traded offered to come in and manage the shop for the two months I would be away. By now Stephen was ready to go back to Sydney as he was missing his family, however, he said he would stay on to take care of the dog, the pool, and the house. "Just go!" he urged me. Len had sent me all the details, the costs, weather, our itinerary, etc.

I left Perth on 1st March and it was 30°C. 22 hours later I arrived at Heathrow, and it was -2°! I was freezing, but I didn't care! I loved London immediately, and I still do!

Len was there to meet me and I was happy to see him. It had been a few years since I had even spoken to him. We had a meal of fish and chips and then headed off up to Walthamstow where I was to stay with my friends the Harrises, and Len went back down south to his father at Tumbridge Wells.

Mrs Harris' son took me up to Petticoat Lane where I bought long socks, a beanie and gloves. I immediately put them on there in the street standing behind a stall. The Harris family were good to me and I loved them all. I had a connection to their son, daughter-in-law and grandchild, Kylie, Mike and Joy, who lived in Perth. Mrs Harris had been out to Australia the previous year and she had spent a couple of nights with me.

"I can't believe June's here, I can't believe June's here!" she kept saying, I had a memorable time with her, mostly gossiping and cups of tea, and suddenly it was a week later and Len turned up to collect me for our tour of the Continent. He had been down to Tunbridge Wells with his dad, who was well into his 80s, and while he was there Len had bought an old car and so we set off on our exciting journey, my first trip on the continent, and what a trip it was.

The boat trip from Dover to Calais was just so incredible. I stood out on deck. It must have been freezing, but I didn't feel cold. This was something I shall never forget, watching the white cliffs of Dover slowly fade into the distance, a different experience altogether to the approach back to Dover from Calais across the Strait of Dover. I can still remember that feeling, the elated excitement.

Our next stop was Paris. Yes, I was in Paris; The Louvre, the Eiffel Tower and the French. The French who did not like tourists. We were okay until we spoke, especially Len with his very proper English accent! However, we got by and I was ready for adventure.

I really got with it in Paris. I swanked around the streets in a green beret pulled down over one ear and thought I looked very Parisian! I loved Paris and promised myself I would go back there with a romantic man on my arm one day in the future. I count my blessings for my memories of my stay in Paris. We headed off the next morning to the coast and Caen; St Lo and Le Mont St Michel.

Mont St Michel is right off the coast and at low tide you can walk out to this old castle that has been converted into a miniature township, which also catered to overnight accommodation, so we spent a night there. I was enthralled with this unique place. From memory it was very hilly with cobblestone streets and every conceivable type of shop within this old castle. As we walked up this steep hill looking at all the touristy shops we came to a butcher shop.

I stopped to look in the window and here was this enormous dog sitting in behind the counter. "Oh my god!" I said to Len, "That's enough for me, I'll never eat meat again!"

And true to my word, it was 16 years before red meat passed my lips again. However, eventually I did need to give up my "no red meat", and that's another story for another day. In the morning we had to wait for the tide to turn before we could set off on the next leg of our journey. Mont St Michel was an experience I have never forgotten.

From there we went to Rennes, Nantes and Bordeaux. We had aimed at crossing the border into Spain over the Pyrenees Mountains before dark. As we travelled towards the border soldiers confronted us with rifles drawn, but I don't remember any great fear even though this was the first time I had had such an experience.

These soldiers searched our car, checked our passports and waved us on. I couldn't speak a word of the language and was glad to be out of there and on our way again.

I was glad to leave the French countryside behind for one reason only. I really wasn't impressed with the families relieving themselves, all side by side, on the edge of the road, with their bare bottoms facing us. It was obviously quiet acceptable in France at that time, but I did not find it acceptable behaviour. Neither was my recollection of when we were in an upmarket restaurant in Paris and I went to the toilet. When I came out of the toilet and went to wash my hands I glanced sideways and here was this man washing his hands in the basin beside me. I hurried out of there as quick as I could

I said to Len, "Can you believe this, I went into the

men's toilet?"

He laughed, "No, June, they all go in together here, they're a funny lot these froggies!"

Crossing the Pyrenees was a memorable experience for me. I loved the countryside and the excitement of another country. These countries all seemed so different and yet so close to each other and the scenery was always changing. We arrived at Jaca late at night and it was freezing cold. We were hungry and as it happened we didn't have any Spanish currency. The clerk on the desk of the only hotel in town couldn't speak English. Somehow he made us understand that he would only let us stay the night if we gave him our passports, just until we got some local money the next day.

Eventually and with much trepidation we handed our passports over to him, as we didn't really have any option. It was the only time on the trip that I felt fearful. Needless to say our passports were given back to us the next morning.

After I settled down from having been accosted with rifles and having my passport taken I found I liked Spain, as the Spanish were more relaxed and helpful, at least when I could make them understand me. We had a kitty for our daily expenses, which we replenished each night with money for the next day. We would both put $20 in the little tin. It seems impossible now that $40 paid for our petrol, food and accommodation on most days. I was chief treasurer.

By now we had it all down to a fine art. We would have breakfast in our room before we set off and by mid-morning we knew we had to find a bakery for our daily loaf and whatever else we needed, as they all closed up shop at midday and went home to bed for siesta. We had to be prepared or by the time we were ready for lunch the shops would all be closed. Around three o'clock in the afternoon we started looking for accommodation for the night. I had acquired the art of approaching a local with my head on the side and my hands joined under my head. I usually managed to find someone who understood my body language. "I want to eat and sleep!"

The restaurants all closed until around 10pm. We soon got sick of sitting around waiting for them to open so we could have our dinner, so we decided to buy a primus and a couple of saucepans and have a try at cooking our evening meal. This certainly had its drawbacks. Trying to read the labels on the tins was a problem. I was always worried we would be eating dog food.

The places we stayed all said "No cooking in the rooms!" I can remember one particular night when we were walking up this steep stairway and Len dropped the bag and the saucepans went clanging down the stairs. I got hysterical, thinking it was just the funniest thing, but not everyone shared my mirth with me and I can't remember if we ate that night.

Jaca was just a border town and I was looking forward to Madrid. What a disappointment I was in for in this city. We drove around and around the city for nearly two hours with me insisting that Len keep trying, but there was nowhere to park and finally we gave up and left. We travelled on to Valencia where we spent the night by the sea and the scenery was spectacular.

The next morning we were off early for Barcelona, where we spent the night. It was a short day, as I wanted to head off the next morning and spend some money in the little duty-free town of Andorra. Andorra was a bit of a disappointment, however, I managed to buy some really cheap alcohol, but Len was not impressed. He complained I would never get all the booze across the border, and thought there would be trouble.

I stood my ground and when the guards stopped us, because Len was travelling on a British passport, they searched his bags thoroughly, looked at my Australian passport, smiled and waved us on.

"I don't think these froggies like the Poms much!" I gloated.

Of course they didn't know I was taking this alcohol back

to a Pom, my dear friend Mrs Harris in England.

One of the most exciting events for me on the whole trip was our visit to Albi, and that was our next stop. Albi is the home town of Toulouse Lautrec. The home where he was born has been converted into a gallery for his works. We spent a memorable few hours there and I bought some souvenirs. I have had a fascination with Toulouse Lautrec since I was a young girl. I remember seeing a movie about his life when I was a teenager.

Our next adventure was to be Monaco and the palace and hopefully see a royal or two. I was to be disappointed, for after walking up seemingly hundreds of steps to the pink palace we were to discover that it was closed to the public at that time. "Oh well" I thought "at least I've been here!"

After six weeks on the continent we were both looking forward to some good, old English fish and chips out of the newspaper.

"I know a great place about half an hour up the road after we land," exclaimed Len. Wonderful, I thought, there's nothing like a flask of tea and fish and chips by the roadside. But would you know it? The fish and chip shop was closed, as it did not open on Sundays. No fish and chips that night. It was probably tea and a sandwich.

I had decided I wanted a week in London on my own, so Len dropped me in Sloan Square, where I found a room in Sloan Gardens for a week, and he went off home.

That was a truly wonderful week and I packed a lot into every day. Every night I would write a list of what I would do the next day. Buckingham Palace, the Tower of London, Westminster Abbey, Piccadilly Circus. I really had my skates on.

I love the theatre so I went to see *The Mouse Trap,* and I walked across Waterloo Bridge. This was something I had always wanted to do after seeing the movie *Waterloo Bridge* when I was a young girl.

I have had a lifelong love affair with London and the Royal Family, so the big thing on my agenda for the first day was to go to St Paul's Cathedral. I had read up a lot about Sir Christopher Wren and the cathedral. I was finally walking up the steps. "How exciting this is!" I thought. There was an official at the top of the steps and he was putting up a barricade.

"Sorry, lady," he said to me. "St Paul's is closed today."

I was struck dumb, but not for long, however. I started to cry. "I am from Australia," I said, "and this is my only chance to visit St Paul's Cathedral. It is something I have wanted to do all my life." I don't know if it was my tears or my Aussie accent, but he let me pass.

He said, "Okay, lady, but please don't make any noise, and stay at the back of the cathedral." What a memorable experience it turned out to be. The choir were practising so I sat in the back. I just closed my eyes and listened, and I have never experienced anything like the sound of that choir.

Lady Diana and Prince Charles were to be married there in two months' time, and the choir were actually practising for their Royal Wedding. I didn't realise it at the time, but I was experiencing this before anyone else in the world!

Maybe even before Diana and Charles?

Well I had done what I wanted to do; I'd had my week in London and seen all the things I wanted to see.

I took a quick trip up to see the Harris family, and I promised Mrs Harris I would come back one day, which I did do, and I then set off home to Perth and my business commitments.

Me in France beside the Eiffel Tower.

CHAPTER 24

A GIFT FROM GOD

My niece Kim had come to live in Perth. She had married a WA man and she and Ray were living close to me. Her husband was a very special person and a good husband to Kim. They had a little white toy poodle dog, Zoe. She was quite an old lady, 8 years (56 human years) when I first met her, well past child bearing age, or so we thought! Zoe was having a, what we thought to be, a friendship with a miniature poodle from two doors up. 'Putty' would come to visit her every night with his little bell tinkling around his neck. As it turned out Putty had more than his bell tinkling and before we knew where we were, Zoe was, yes you guessed it, pregnant with a capital P!

On 23rd March, 1983, 2am in the morning, Brendan Kaye, the local vet from Applecross, was called in, as his help was needed to assist Zoe with her delivery. With the help of Brendan, poor old Zoe was to eventually deliver her babies. She was the proud mother of 4 bouncing puppies, 3 boys and a girl. Little did I know, that night would change and enhance my life for many years to come.

Zoe was unable to breastfeed her babies, probably owing to mastitis and of course her advanced years. For weeks it was an endless procession of babies and bottles. One of the most memorable sights for me was seeing Ray, this big, strapping, 6ft man, bottle-feeding these tiny pups. Life was just wonderful in Kim's household for six weeks, however, Ray finally insisted, "Kim, the pups have to be sold, we just can't keep five dogs!"

An advertisement was placed in the local paper. "Pups for sale, against the wishes of their foster grandmother. Fleur, Lincoln, Minuette and Pierrot, they are all beautiful and just six weeks old':

Pierrot had always been Kim's favourite, and when anyone came to buy a dog she would hide him in the toilet, as he was the pick of the litter. Finally Ray said, "This seems strange to me Kim, I thought Pierrot would have been the first to be sold."

"It seems we may have to keep him!" said Kim. A terrible argument broke out, and Kim rang me to relate the sad story. "Aunty June, could you please take Pierrot, just for the weekend, as I need time to talk to Ray. I need to persuade him to keep Pierrot. I could not bear for him to just disappear from my life."

"Well, Kim, you know I could never have a dog. I'm at work all day, I just couldn't think of it," I said. And then I thought, oh well then, just for the weekend, just to help her out. She will have to take him back on Sunday night and I really was a bit put out. "A dog for god's sake, with my busy life!" I thought... After just two days he had found his way into my life and into my heart. I had decided I could not part with this darling little bundle of white fluff.

I had built a protective wall around myself and the building blocks were constructed of work. Up until now I filled my days with running a successful retail business.

I had no balance in my life, only work and grief.

So was the beginning of what turned out to be a blessing

directly from God! As it turned out, Pierrot was my saviour, my life. He gave me so much happiness.

Pierrot enriched my life in every way. It was six years since I had lost my girls and I never wanted to love anything or anyone ever again, but I now had my Pierrot. He went everywhere with me.

I always worried about him being home alone all day. One Saturday morning I decided I would take Pierrot to work with me. He soon became an Arcade identity. Everyone adored him, customers, passers-by and my fellow shop owners, so I took a little antique chair into the shop for him to sit on.

My customers all loved Pierrot. They would try a dress on, come out and say, "Pierrot, do you like me in this?" Or "Pierrot, do you think I look too fat in this dress?" He was a delight. One day I was down on the floor playing with him and laughing happily. I stopped in my tracks. I was stunned. I realised "I have not laughed, really laughed, since the girls died!" At that moment I made a conscious decision to laugh every day from then on, even if I only laughed at myself.

One weekend I was down south at Busselton with Pierrot, buying a pie for myself and one for him for our lunch when two ladies walked passed and said, "Oh look! There's little Pierrot from Centre Way's Arcade!" They came over and gave him a pat, just smiling briefly at me.

I might not have been too well known, but it seemed Pierrot certainly was.

In the 15½ years of his life Pierrot became a seasoned traveller. I flew him from Perth to Sydney and back home again on many occasions. When I went up north to Shark Bay on a fishing trip he flew in the cabin of the light plane with me. He was a real Perth identity.

We caravanned around Australia and finally flew from Perth to Queensland to live

Pierrot passed over on 1st September, 1998. He had had a heart attack six weeks earlier. His veterinary surgeon, Simon

Pace, found that the University of NSW were replacing the heart valves in poodles very successfully. Pierrot was too ill to fly, however, but Stephen, who was then in Queensland working with me in the health shop, agreed to drive us interstate to NSW for the operation. I was desperate!

When Simon inquired further the specialists in Sydney said they were not prepared to take the risk of an operation because of his age. I was devastated.

In retrospect he would not have survived the journey.

I finally made the awful decision. Pierrot was to suffer no longer. I phoned Dawn Chapman. a lady who worked for me for 10 years. She said she would send her Ray to take me to Cleveland to our vet, Simon Pace. Pierrot was to have euthanasia. I sat with him on my lap under the front window waiting for Ray. Pierrot got down from my lap and staggered around to have a last look in every room in the house. He had a look out the back door at his beloved garden and then came to me to pick him up. He was telling me he had had enough. I nursed him and talked to him through it to the end.

Pierrot had a good life and he gave me many years of happiness. His time with me was over.

I brought Pierrot home from the vet and lay him on my bed. My friend Jeanette Bloomfield came and we lay either side of him for several hours.

"Pets at Peace" came and took him away to be cremated. I carried him out to the van and insisted his face be left uncovered so he could lie facing the window. Pierrot always loved to look out the window. His ashes in their little urn were brought back to me the next day.

Pierrot's little urn with his ashes inside sat on my desk for many years.

My little darling had enriched my life for so long. On the 30th anniversary of the girls' death I took his ashes to Pinegrove and buried him with the girls. After sitting on my desk in his little urn for a number of years my darling little person, who had enriched my life for so long, was finally put to rest beside Cathy and Lyndy at Pinegrove.

Me, with my darling Pierrot at Mandurah, Perth.

CHAPTER 25

ENTER THE LOTHARIO

I had been living in Perth for about four years when I met a fine man, one of the nicest men I have ever known, and our relationship extended a couple of years. Looking back now I realise I loved him dearly. He was a deep-sea fisherman but, owing to him being away with his work for months at a time, it was an on/off type of a relationship I guess. He was good for me, he could make me laugh–get me out of myself. But as usual in most relationships, there was a big problem. He was married; his wife had been in a psychiatric hospital for many years, and I often felt he carried a lot of guilt. She had given birth to five children in as many years and perhaps this had helped to push her over the edge. They had not lived as man and wife for many years; however, from time to time he brought her home for short spells.

Here I was with this big, six-foot, virile man. I called him my Greek God, and I believed at the time we were both "a wonderful relationship looking for somewhere to happen."

He would sometimes comment, "June, I guess I will turn up one day and you will say, 'go away, I'm getting married'!" He only had one daughter. She was a nursing sister and had a new baby and he adored them both. He often said she would never accept him having anyone in his life. So for that reason I never told him I loved him. I always thought "I don't want to be in a situation, where I have caused a rift between a man and his children." What a fool I was!

One of his sons used to sell fish in the arcade where I had my boutique, and he would run around selling these trays of wonderful fresh seafood.

I remember one day Carmel, a young woman who worked part-time for me, saying, "Wow, what a sort!" I smiled to myself thinking "Oh yes and you should see his father!"

It was a relationship that did not sit well with me. I was very, very lonely and I wanted someone who was there for me, there at Christmas, birthdays and a mate to spend my weekends with.

Yes, his prediction came true. I did meet someone and he was sent on his way.

A couple of years later his son came into the shop and said "Oh, by the way, Dad's alone now and he's living up north on a small farm; I thought you might like to know." I was stunned. I realised he must have told his son about me, about our relationship.

I quickly explained to him that I was getting married in a couple of weeks. I never knew if the poor woman had died, or maybe he had just had enough and finally made the break. However, I was shattered! The man I still loved dearly was free and obviously alone, and here I was getting married in two weeks to someone I did not love. I grew to love him and yet, I was never in love with him. In time I grew to loathe him.

When I was growing up, my mum had always told me. "You never, never, ever have more than one man in your life at a time" and I never did. But I was not so sure that she gave me the best of advice.

Yes, this new man came into my life, and he decided he was there to stay. He was 6 foot and 18 stone, with a weak mouth; he was unattractive in every way. However, he had the gift of the gab and an iron will. He wined me and dined me. He brought me flowers and chocolates, and the bullshit flowed non stop.

I was ruthless with him; I told him I did not like fat men. He went on a strict diet and the weight fell off him. He lost I don't know how many stone in a matter of months.

I told him he drank too much coffee, as in my opinion 20 cups a day was excessive. He stopped drinking coffee that day and he never touched it again. Now this could be seen to be a man in love, just trying to please. However, I often wondered, "was he someone with a sick determination, who would go to any extreme to get what he wanted?"

I would send him on his way and tell him I did not want to see him again. I was cruel, but truthful; I continually told him I didn't want him in my life. But then, when I would arrive home from work he'd be sitting on my doorstep the next night, with flowers and, "Darling, I have booked the Garden Room Restaurant at the Parmelia for dinner."

Loneliness makes us vulnerable and in the ensuing years I eventually came to terms with the reality that he was a man who stalked vulnerable women. And I was to see him do this many times, to many, many women: sometimes to close friends of mine.

When I first met him I had been living alone for nearly 10 years. He told me he had been widowed for two years and I had no cause to doubt him. After a short time he took me to meet his family. His son was a very special man and I grew very fond of him. On this first family meeting it somehow came out that their mother, his wife, had been dead for only six months. She had actually died on my Cathy's birthday.

I was appalled and stunned. Why would he lie about a thing

like that? And so my life went down a track of living with lies and deception. One Saturday evening I was all dressed to go out for dinner with him. Six o'clock came and went 6.30, 7.30, 8 and 8.30.

Finally it was almost 9pm and he knocked on the door. He had tears in the eyes, flowers, and some cock and bull story about a lady friend of the family whose daughter was in hospital with appendicitis,

This young girl wanted only to see her beloved uncle. She did not want her mother or father, only himself. Now, he had spoken often about this woman many times, but I was yet to meet her.

I was spitting chips! But all I said was, "You will do this to me but once, if it ever happens again I will not open the door to you. If necessary I'll have you removed from my premises." He was never late again. We went out to dinner and of course the whole evening was a disaster.

He did everything to hold me. He loved my darling Pierrot, I have to admit, but then everyone loved Pierrot! On Pierrot's second birthday he bought him pale blue monogrammed towels with his name on them. Nothing was too good for Pierrot or myself, and the bull flowed out of his mouth. Yes he was a gifted bullshit artist. However, this woman always seemed to be in the background, and one day he phoned me at work to say he was bringing her into the city to meet me. I will always remember that day; she had a bunch of carnations in her hand, presumably for me, or maybe he had bought them for her, I had no idea. But as we sat there in the coffee shop he introduced us, himself and herself on one side of the table, and me on the other, she actually threw these carnations on to the table in front of me and said nothing! We engaged in some small talk for a while, drank our coffee, and I then got up to go back to work. I left them sitting there together and I had this sick apprehension come over me.

I wondered was I letting myself in for more heartbreak

with this man of many faces. I might add I left the carnations on the table where they had been thrown. I have never liked carnations anyway. I'm a lady who loves roses.

About a year later her son was getting married and of course "Uncle had to be the MC." When the dreaded day arrived we were seated at the bridal table and she was sitting next to himself and she actually laid on his shoulder most of the night. I was just so humiliated! And I wondered why her husband was tolerating this blatant expression of a seemingly clandestine liaison? And yes, why was I tolerating it? I realise now, my confidence and self-esteem were being slowly but surely chipped away.

I had been going out with him for about a year, but it had not been the best of years and I had a lot of doubts about him and our relationship. He wanted me to go up to Hong Kong with him for a holiday. I didn't know what to do; will I? won't I? In the end, and after a lot of pressure from him, I decided I would go. We had an absolutely wonderful time.

Time passed, and suddenly it was two years since we had first met and he was still very much in the picture. He wanted to get married and I was vulnerable as I had been on my own a long time and we were getting along okay at this time. Finally we decided to jointly buy this dilapidated old house on the river at Applecross. I put my skills, heart and soul into renovating and restoring the old house and I turned it into a beautiful home. When the renovations were completed our home was just wonderful.

Finally we were to be married. A condition of the marriage was that she was not to be invited; strangely enough he complied with my desire with very little opposition. But then I had given him an ultimatum "If she's there, I won't be!"

However, this was really not a great problem to him and there were so many other women for me to contend with over the duration of the marriage.

One morning, a couple of months after we were married,

I had remained in bed with a migraine headache. During the course of the morning I got up for some reason and as I walked down the hall I thought "That's unusual for our hall glass door to be closed, it's always open." The next moment I remember standing looking through the door and here he was with this woman, our neighbour, in his arms! What happened next is completely lost to me, and to this day I still know nothing of the next 15 or so hours. The next thing I knew it was midnight, and I was down sitting on the water's edge hysterical.

He didn't come near me, or try to help me.

Apparently I had been in shock and had completely lost 15 hours of my life. But strangely enough the matter was never discussed, just left to fester in my heart.

After much thought and discussion we decided to buy a caravan and start touring around, as this was something I was really keen to do. The marriage wasn't particularly happy and I realise now that my thoughts at that time were "If he's with me in a caravan he has less chance of womanising," but you can't run away from your problems, you always take them with you wherever you go. We had some wonderful adventures and many a night of smuggling my darling Pierrot into NO DOGS caravan parks, and of course once a week when he was due for his bath, I made him wrap Pierrot in a towel and smuggle him into a shower.

We set off up the West Australian coast, spent a week in Broome and then on to Darwin, over the top of Australia and eventually down the Queensland coast to Brisbane. I was looking forward to seeing my dear friend Jan who had left Perth a short time before.

She had gone to settle and live in Raby Bay in Brisbane, Queensland on the canals. This visit was to cause another dramatic change in my life.

Jan begged us to stay on with her, and as she was to spend Christmas alone we decided to stay. We were out walking along the ocean one day when we came across a house for sale. We decided to have an inspection. It was a dream of a home and we fell in love with it. The long and the short of it all was, we put a deposit on the house and flew home to Perth two days later. We put our house in Perth on the market the next day and it was sold the day after that. We were back living in Queensland within six weeks.

After the house was sold and we were packing up to move, I looked around me at the beautiful home I had created out of a crumbling wreck and then I glanced over at himself. He was standing looking out the window at the river and of course he had the ever-ready tears in the eyes. I quietly explained, "Yes, have a good look around, see what we are leaving behind us, and remember, if you carry on in this next house the way you did in this one, it will go to the same grave. I poured my heart into this place, but I have hated it since that day, the day I found you with Evelyn!" He didn't even answer me. And of course leopards don't change their spots. We certainly took our troubles with us. When trust and respect goes out of a marriage there is really not much left in it.

The beautiful house on the ocean in Queensland went to the same grave. It took a few years longer, but it went there just the same.

When I had my boutique in Perth, one of my friends had saved a little money and had purchased a unit for herself, but it was a mess, so himself and I volunteered to help her with the cleaning and painting.

I didn't last long, as the work was too hard and heavy for me, but he continued to help her, and after a while I started to wonder? He was going out a lot at night.

One night out of curiosity I drove to her house and sure enough his car was in the drive. The house was in darkness except for a small light in her bedroom.

I had keys to his car on my key ring and I remember sitting there thinking "I will drive his car through her bedroom window!"

I don't know where I was coming from. I feel sure it wasn't

a jealousy thing, just humiliation, and for the first time in my life I had serious competition and lots of it. I had grown up an only girl and my Dad's little darling and I always felt special. I had had two previous husbands, and they both adored me. I suppose I had always been the "Queen Bee." Well, with this monster I was brought down to earth with a jolt.

I guess I should have confronted him, but I didn't. I just kept sweeping it under the carpet. I should have realised our problems were never going to go away.

It took a long time and professional help for me to move away from this dreadful man. To remove this monster from my life! There were so many women who floated in and out of our lives. I could write a whole book on his womanising, yes, just on this subject alone. I had known him 7 years and been married to him for 5.

I really put it all away so long ago. I have moved on. None of it is of any importance to me any more. I have removed him from my reality.

One really close friend in particular, Jan (she used to call me her soul mate) chose to listen to his lies.

I have always believed, when it comes to intimate, close friends, one should never have to justify oneself. If they are worth their salt they will stick by you. But she did not! No doubt today she would know what a terrible injustice she did me at that time.

But then, there was a time when I fell for his lies. All he really was, was just a big, heavy, cumbersome load of bullshit that spewed its vileness over into society!

My life with this man was years of sheer hell.

Many times I said to him, "You are the only totally bad person I have ever known!" There was never any answer. If you don't speak you can't incriminate yourself seemed to be his philosophy.

After what I had been through in my life, meeting him just seemed to be so unfair. Surely I deserved something better than this monster!

Once, while living in Perth, I tried to talk to my friend about him. I went to see her. I was an emotional mess that day. She did not believe me. She could not understand. He had everyone fooled, this seemingly wonderful man. I never again attempted to talk to anyone about my problems with him. I just bottled it up year after year. I thought if my dear friend didn't believe me no-one would.

There were literally dozens of women who floated in and out of his life… our lives. No-one could believe this man, the double life he lived! It wasn't until after the break-up that I finally found someone who knew him as I did. His own son.

I rang him one night and said, "Your father and I have parted and he says he is going to commit suicide, and I can't help him. Would you please fly over here? I think it is unfair to give you my side of the story. I am prepared to talk this out with him present."

Well what a shock I was in for. His son's answer to me was, "No, June, I won't be coming. There is nothing you can tell me about him that I don't already know." We talked for an hour and he told me what a terrible life his mother had had. He related to me all the lies and deceit that had gone on when they had come to Australia to live from Northern Ireland.

He said, "When you were getting married the family discussed whether or not we should have a talk to you about him?" To my detriment they decided against that line of action! He went on to explain, "We thought well, she's a good woman, and maybe she will straighten him out."

Mission Impossible!

From the time I got him out of the house it was two and half years before I finally got him out of my life. Two and a half years of hell and many restraining orders. Plus I was supporting him and paying rent on a unit for him. After we had broken up my friend rang me at work one day and said, "He is going to commit suicide. You must help him."

I said, "I can't, I'm working." I got off the phone and started to worry, and then I decided to ring the local police and ask them to go and check on him. An hour later they rang back.

"Oh he's fine." they said. He was mowing the lawn and had made a joke of the whole thing.

I remember one day a young police prosecutor came up to me at the court and quietly whispered, "Born into violence, they live to hate."He could have been speaking about anyone, but I knew exactly who he meant.

I must say the many police who were in my life at that period in time were wonderful to me. Really, I would not have so many problems today. For women like me the stalking laws were not available in those days. I remember one time I went to the local police as he had come into the house and ejaculated on the hand towel I always kept on the wash-basin.

The police asked me, "What was the make and number of his car?" I told them, and yes they had him under surveillance as a suspected robber or a peeping Tom! The neighbours had complained about him.

Today it's called stalking and it carries a jail sentence.

My son-in-law said to me one day, "June, the bad times are like the good times, they don't last for ever." This was true; this terrible time in my life finally came to an end.

However, my health suffered. I weighed only 48 kg and my normal weight was 60 kg and my finances suffered greatly.

I went into that marriage owning two properties and a viable business.

I came out of it with a struggling business and $20,000.

I was not physically or mentally strong enough to go to court to fight for my rightful share.

I had to start again, living in an awful rented house, and virtually penniless. But I had some fight and energy still left in me to build the business and I worked for 10 years virtually night and day, to finally retire. My life today is uneventful I guess, but it's good.

CHAPTER 26

QUEENSLAND RETAILER OF THE YEAR

We had been living in Queensland for a short time, and as we had done a lot of travelling, we both felt the need to be doing something more with our lives, and earning some money. Neither of us had been successful with our job applications. My problem was that my self-confidence and self-esteem had been destroyed. I thought we could perhaps think about going into retailing, as I knew I could make that work.

After looking around for several months, we finally settled on a health shop reasonably close to home. I should have had the foresight to realise that he was not a people-person. He just didn't have any people skills, only womanising skills. He was hopeless in the business, he continually insulted the carriers and began banning certain companies from the shop. What a nightmare my life had become! When the stock stopped coming into the store and I phoned our suppliers to find out why, and where were our deliveries, it was always the same answer. Their deliverymen had been banned from the premises. A lot of the customers also disliked him. He hated the shop. And the atmosphere was dreadful He was good for floating around the shopping centre, doing the banking, unpacking stock, when we managed to get it, and weighing up food. I became the workhorse.

One morning he was going to the bank. I called, "Hang on, I might come with you for a walk." When we got near the bank he told me to wait outside for him. That's all he said, "You wait outside." I did not have the confidence to confront him. I just went back to work and did some "head-talk" to myself for the remainder of the day about what was probably going on with one of the girls in the bank.

I recalled some years before when we were in the city and he had to go into a building to collect a cheque for some work he had done. When we reached the building he had snapped, "You wait down here, go and look at the shops!" Even though I knew he had something going on in there, I did as I was told. I hated myself for being so weak.

Within a year of buying the business the marriage was over, but I was determined to hang on to the business. He was hell bent on forcing me to sell it. I knew we would not get our money back as we had already done a new fit-out. We were behind the eight-ball. For once I won, but at a terrible financial loss to me. However, I knew if I could stay there and work hard, I would one day be out of debt and own my own home again. I was living in dreadful rented premises at the time.

It took over two years to get this enigma out of my life and out of my business. After that I went from strength to strength, even though it took me 10 years, 10 long years of working, 6 days a week in the store and the never-ending bookwork after hours.

The store was now one of a nationwide chain, and it went from strength to strength.

In the early days we had our monthly meetings in a grotty room at Stones Corner. We carried our sandwiches and coffee up this great flight of stairs. This didn't go down well with me after standing on my feet all day.

I started plugging away at Richard, our Director here in Queensland. "Richard, we are a growing concern, a force to be reckoned with. We should be meeting at the best venues in Brisbane." He agreed with me and it did eventuate.

I'm sure he found me a "pain in the bum." I really put him through his paces. I was always interjecting and interrupting during our meetings, generally having too much to say. Our Richard was a real chauvinist. Not a chauvinist pig, just a chauvinist!

At one particular meeting, I interrupted him. "Richard, there is something I wish to address the group about, is that possible?"

He replied, "Yes, June, you can have five minutes!" Well, talk about a "red rag to a bull!"

I stood up, hands on hips. "Richard, you have held the floor for the last hour, and you're giving me five minutes. You are the limit!"

One particular incident stands out in my mind. When we were at our yearly conference at a new hotel on the Gold Coast, Richard's wife, Cuti, had been asked to give a speech about something or other. She was a wonderful speaker and left us all enthused and motivated.

I was having coffee with Richard and a couple of other colleagues during the break when he declared, "I never realised my wife was such a good speaker. I'm amazed!"

"Well, Richard, that's because you never give her a chance to open her mouth." I laughed. I certainly never learnt to keep my mouth shut.

Even with all the flak he had taken from me demanding the women be allowed to have a turn at chairing the meetings, etc, I know he always held me in very high esteem.

I, in turn, thought the world of Richard. He had all our interests at heart. He was an achiever of the highest calibre. He will always hold a special place in my heart.

I have never regretted retiring from work. However, I have missed my bantering with Richard at our monthly meetings. Also, there are all my wonderful customers.

After I retired Richard and Cuti invited me as guest of honour to the Healthy Life Christmas party.

Another of my colleagues who was special to me was Mike. I remember at a meeting one time, the women were all talking about their children. It was around the time of an anniversary of the death of my girls. Mike came and sat next to me, put his arm around me and whispered, "It's not fair, June, the women are thoughtless, I feel for you at this time." Mike was a darling person, he had empathy for me and he showed it.

When the weather was cool I would usually take Pierrot to the meetings with me, as he was so easy, so placid. He would sit on the front seat of my car on his lambs wool rug, and when Alan or Mike were going outside for a smoko they would pick up my car keys, and give Pierrot a cuddle and a wee-wee walk and probably a nibble from our dinner table.

One year I won the award of Queensland Retailer Of The Year. This was an extremely prestigious award. The presentation was in Sydney and held at the function rooms of Royal Randwick Racecourse. I was in shock when they called my name and I had to take my place on the stage. I had my first experience with stage fright. I could not speak for several minutes. However, I soon took the mike and did myself and my staff proud. Part of my speech was "Any business is only as successful as your staff make it."

The manager of David Jones in Sydney made this same statement, many years earlier. No truer words have ever been spoken.

That same year my store won the local newspaper award in the category of Health and Fitness.

We must have been doing something right. And with himself out of the business we could not but succeed.

Then in 1996 Stephen came to Queensland to work in the

business with me and he started keeping company with Sandy, one of my staff. Three years later when the business was to be sold they went back to Sydney together,

They married at Christmas 2000.

Stephen was long overdue for some happiness, and I know he has found it at last with Sandy. She plays golf with him, goes on his motorbike-club trips, she is a great cook and housekeeper and gardener.

Like he once said, "The bad times like the good times don't last for ever."

I'm sure he is having his good times now.

He deserves all the happiness in the world.

My staff and I had a genuine bonding with our customers. We had an exceptionally loyal clientele. They made life and all my hard work rewarding, but of course we had our share of odd bods. I recall one evening, it was nearly 6pm and I was exhausted, making up the till. This woman pushed our door open, waltzed in as if it was 10am and demanded, "Do you have any gluten-free biscuits?" I pointed to them on the counter. "Don't be so stupid, they're not gluten free." she shouted. This was just too much at the end of a long day. She then continued to look around the store, in the fridge, etc. Then she came up to me and declared, "So, you don't have any gluten-free food?"

"No," I snapped, "Stupid people don't sell gluten-free food!"

She was back in the next day, large as life.

That was one of the rare occasions when "the customer wasn't always right."

We also sold health and beauty magazines. I had a new shipment on the counter and the flavour of that month was "Herbs to improve your sex life."

One morning a couple of regulars came in. I don't think they were married, and neither of them was very bright, but good customers. They usually came in a couple of times a week. The first thing she noticed was the new mags. And she honed in on them, she grabbed one, shoved it in his face and shrieked, "Look, look, this is what you need, maybe this will help you! Buy it, buy it!" Now, he had a set, determined expression on his face. He took the mag from her, placed it firmly on the counter and muttered, "No. I have told you before; you're wasting our time. Now just forget about it."

She stood there pouting. The subject was closed. In moments like this, the staff always managed to disappear and leave me to handle it. We had many a long and hearty laugh. Sometimes it verged on hysteria.

There were also the sad cases… grandmothers having to cope with their darling grandchildren being molested by their stepfathers. Watching young women waste away with Anorexia Nervosa. The really sad cases were men, women and children dying with cancer. It was all in a day's work.

CHAPTER 27

LOOKING BACK

Looking back now, I believe my life has been like a tree that has been nurtured in good soil with lots of love and affection. A tree that stands up straight, withstands all the hurricanes, bad weather and whatever comes along.
A tree nurtured and grown in good soil is hard to destroy.

Because I was reared with such loving care, it has helped me to withstand all the tragedies and hardships that have touched my life.

* * *

14th Feb 2002.

Today, I have come to terms with the fact of life; the girls did not just die. I have never before been able to think this through completely. I have always just said and thought "they died" like they went away. I have now come to terms with the truth. They were crushed to death in the Granville Train Disaster.

A short time after the Granville Rail Disaster, Sir Eric Willis, the then NSW Minister for Transport, announced to the people of Sydney, via radio, "Don't drive your cars to the city, use public transport, THE RAILWAY IS THE SAFE WAY." I was angry. I told people, "I should get a gun and shoot that bastard." I soon found myself in Concord Repat Hospital Psychiatric Ward. It was a mixed ward, male and female, where the inmates were either senile or mentally disturbed.

One old lady persisted in taking off all her clothes and running around the ward screaming all night. What a dreadful place for me to be. I knew all about mental institutions from the past experience with my first husband. I was terrified they would give me shock treatment. My stepson Steven, would come and sit with me for hours, what an awful experience for a young man. After a couple of days I was taken to see the resident psychiatrist, Dr Beverley Raphael. Beverley is a lovely, compassionate lady. She had been at the scene of the Granville Rail Disaster, counselling the injured and their families. Beverley spoke with me for a short time, then she burst into tears. She could not help me so it seemed. There is just so much one can take, and psychiatrists are no exception. They are human beings too! Sydney was a city in shock, all of Australia was. People across the world were shocked. As time went on I found it was easier for people to walk away than to reach out. For many years I felt a complete and utter outcast from society. Of all the friend and relatives I had, I can honestly say that only a very few people were there for me at that time. I wish to name them here; they were Fred and Lynne Bastian, Helen Dalrymple, Stephen, my son-in-law and Steven Kells, my stepson. I shall hold them in my heart until the day I die.

I was in Concord for about a week. My GP was instrumental in my release. He knew Concord was not the place for me to be, however, that was not to be my last encounter with such an experience.

CHAPTER 28

THE THIRTY-YEAR MEMORIAL

In December 2006 I had been living in Queensland for nearly 20 years. I kept thinking I should go down to Granville for the 30-year memorial. It was 10 years since I had been down to a memorial. I went through weeks of should I go?

I can't do it.

I should go.

No, it is too hard.

I am not up to it.

I remember when Stephen and I went down for the 20th anniversary. I don't remember shedding a tear! However, I do remember afterwards Stephen saying, "June, I will never go there again. We should never have put ourselves through that."

I had talked about it to friends and had decided not to go. However, it was still in the back of my mind, haunting me.

On Tuesday, the morning of 16th January, I awoke feeling strong and positive. I decided if I could get myself organised that day I would go down to Sydney the next day. It would be the day before the Granville Train Disaster 30-year memorial.

I phoned my friend Helen Dalrymple. Helen gave me the phone number of a good hotel in Parramatta, The Sebel. I phoned them and made a tentative booking for the 17th-20th January. My first priority was my dog, Monet. Everything fell into place. A friend, Jan Box, readily agreed to have him. On this day I was in a state of anxiety, but very positive. I did not hesitate. I had made up my mind and I was going, if everything fell into place. It did. However, reflecting back, I did not say to anyone why I was going to Sydney. I did not say Parramatta or Granville. I just said I wanted to go down south. It was like if I mentioned the word Granville I might fall apart. (It comes to me now; if anyone ever asked me where I originated from I have always said NSW or the Western Suburbs of Sydney. If they push it I say the Parramatta area. It is too painful to say the word Granville.)

I had no problems booking a flight. I felt happy having made this decision.

On the previous Sunday I was upset, really in a mess. Another friend, Eileen Cusack, had called me that day, as she was aware of this being an emotional time for me. Eileen is 84 and is a ball of energy. She not only runs everywhere, she also drives everywhere. On Tuesday evening she rang me again. I told her I was off to Sydney the next day. She said, "I will take you to the airport and I will be there to collect you when you return."

In all the years I have never had anyone offer to take me to the airport. I have always had to take a cab or my own car. I was so pleased to have this support. Yes, everything had fallen into place.

On the morning of Wednesday, 17th January, Eileen called for me. We dropped Monet off at Jan's place on the way to the airport. And so I was off, with no thought of the outcome of my trip.

On the flight down I was still anxious. I took a cab from

the airport to Parramatta. It felt great to be back in my home State.

The trip out from the airport to the Western Suburbs brought back a flood of memories. That part of Sydney is very old, and after being away from it for 28 years, living in Perth and Queensland, the streets seemed really derelict.

I must have been in a rather reflective mood that day. I have been back home many, many times. It had been only three years since my last trip.

I have never looked at it in a critical way, really seen it, but then in the past I have always picked up a hire car. Maybe that makes a difference.

I was reflecting on how I had moved up in the world, improved my lifestyle and myself. I have never had a problem with my roots. I came from the Western Suburbs and that was that.

My thoughts were with my friends, Helen, Lyn and Fred. Before I moved to Perth they were incredible. They helped me so much in those crucial years. I was thinking how I have in a lot of ways moved on, done a lot with my life. I was in a very reflective mood.

I arrived at The Sebel, situated at 350 Church Street, Parramatta. The porter took my luggage. I paid the cabbie, stood on the street and looked around me. I was gob smacked.

The Sebel to my amazement is situated opposite Prince Alfred Park. The park the girls and I would often walk through to school and to Mass on Sundays. The park where Cathy had first met Father Mark. A tearful eventful meeting and a wonderful friendship evolved, for she and Stephen with Father Mark from that meeting.

Father Frank had refused to marry Cathy and Stephen because they would not be able to have children. Cathy told Father Mark about this and he said they could wait 6 months and he would marry them in the Catholic Church and Cathy could start taking the sacraments again.

The park had had a wonderful facelift over the years; it now had white roses around the whole perimeter and walkways to the church. St Patrick's Cathedral, where we attended Mass, Cathy and Stephen were married there and the girls were buried from there. When I looked to the right I could see the college the girls attended, Our Lady of Mercy College, and their old primary school, St Patrick's. Two blocks along Victoria Road was the house where the girls grew up. The hotel was situated overlooking the Parramatta River. From my room I could see the bridge I have written about where we could cross from David Jones to take a short cut home across Victoria Road. After I checked in, I sat at my bedroom window reflecting, stunned. It was just incredible. I hadn't thought about where the hotel was situated when I made the booking. I was back in the past with all my beautiful memories of my girls, and also some sadness. However, I did not feel overly sad.

It was mid-afternoon. I had a shower and a rest. I then went out exploring, reminiscing. I walked to the corner, turned into Victoria Road and headed towards my old home; the home my dad had bought for the girls, himself and me in 1966 after Mum passed away. I sat on the fence of the house across the road, looking at our old home, 66 Victoria Road, Parramatta. Sitting on the fence of the house that once belonged to the old lady, the one who had given me so much valuable information about that fatal day 30 years before, when I was on that obsessive mission. My mission was to track down the events of that fateful morning, 18th January, 1977.

The house was unchanged in structure. The carport was still there. The carport where my very first new car, my 1967 blue Holden, the car I was so proud of, once stood. Sadly, the house was very neglected.

Thirty years had paid its toll on our old home.

I wanted to cross the road, walk in and wander around my old garden. I was in a strange mood. I wandered back to the hotel.

I was starving hungry. I hadn't eaten since breakfast. I ordered room service, sat by the window, gazing down at the Parramatta River while I ate my dozen oysters and reflected on the past.

Until I came home it did not occur to me that I had not felt sad that afternoon. My mood was simply reflective, looking back on the past. I was actually enjoying my day. I think it was just as well. I could have slipped back into my old 30-year habit of "I should not be contented or happy. I should be sad." I later phoned Helen to say I had arrived and I would see her in the morning. I had a wonderful sleep, which is unusual for me in a strange bed.

I thought about Helen and the part she played in, I would go so far to say saving, if not my life, at least saving me in those devastating months after the death of the girls.

On the morning of the 18th January I awoke early. I had a large breakfast and wandered out to the foyer to wait for Helen. I had decided we would catch a taxi over to St Mark's Church in Granville where the Memorial Service was to begin. The taxi driver got lost and we arrived just in time for the service. We found a seat towards the front of the church which was completely full. The police, ambulance, fire rescue people. Many of the men and women who attended were on duty on that day 30 years before. The Premier of NSW Peter Debnam, was there. This was the first time in 30 years a Premier had attended. It has always been a sore point. They have always been too busy. The Train Disaster has always been an event the NSW Government has treated as something that never really happened.

Still today there is a contingent that say, "It never really happened." It's easier than hanging their heads in shame.

I still find it heart wrenching to think about the day of the Memorial. The ceremony in the church went on and on. I just sobbed my heart out all the way through. For the first time in

30 years I did not try to hide or suppress my grief. I just gave way to it. The speakers all seemed to be speaking about the accident. This word filled me with so much anger. I wanted to stand and scream out. Accident! It was no accident!

Call it murder! Call it neglect, call it a disaster, call that event what you like. Don't ever call it an accident. It was no accident. It should never have happened.

After the service, which lasted an hour or more, everyone filed out of the church. The NSW police band led the procession through the streets of Granville, followed by the ambulance officers, fire rescue squad and then came the relatives and friends of the deceased and injured. The march finished at the rose garden where the Memorial granite stone rests a few metres from the scene, after being placed there 10 years earlier. The stone has the 83 names of the deceased engraved on it.

As we walked through the streets of Granville, Channel 9 followed beside me with their camera right in my face, and a journalist with the photographer kept asking me for my story. I was too distressed. I could not form words. I could not speak.

Helen came to my rescue and said, "My friend is a private person. She lost her two daughters in the disaster. She does not wish to speak to the press." I must admit they respected my wishes. They moved away and they did not put that segment to air.

Then the local newspapers were asking me for a story. That was not my way. It was like the day of the funeral. I was so fearful that day. I still remember praying the press would not be there at the church.

The whole service seemed to go on for hours. It was 36 degrees and we were standing in the sun most of the time. At the site the speeches started all over again. I don't remember anything much about what was said.

Afterwards everyone wandered up to the town hall for cool drinks and refreshments. Helen fluttered around mixing with and talking to people. I sat in a corner and waited for her. After a time a chap arrived with a box of books and started selling them. The book was called The Granville Train Disaster, by Dan Monty. It was launched that day. I decided to buy a book. I put it on my lap and thought, "It's probably about all the technicalities of the disaster. I will read it when I get home." I'm glad I did not open it until I came home to Queensland. Some days later I opened it and there were not only photos of my girls, but parts of my manuscript as well.

It had been an oppressive, exhausting day for me. We left the town hall and wandered down into town. I went into a florist, purchased two red roses and we went back to the site where I placed them among all the other floral tributes that had been left there that day.

We caught a cab and returned to the hotel. I had a shower and a nap. I was exhausted. Helen curled up in a chair and chatted away to me about our day.

I felt refreshed and at peace after my rest. We decided to wander up town and have a meal. I kept thinking how "at peace" I felt. I slept well again that night, no dreams, no tears.

It had been arranged that the next day, Helen's daughter, Sherry, would take us to visit Pinegrove Memorial Gardens where the girls were buried. We decided to set off about 8am to beat the heat of the day.

I was out of bed, showered and had eaten early. I was very aware of my feeling of peace. I felt light and tranquil. I wandered out on to the street, decided to walk through Prince Alfred Park and over to St Pat's and around my girls' old school. I still had this feeling of calm and peace with me. The park's facelift was really something. So many people were using it these days. I did think "if I had not gone away to Perth I would possibly know some of these people wandering through our park."

I was heading back to the hotel when I noticed across the other side of the walkway a gardener was trimming the beautiful white rose bushes. Amazingly, when I was a child we had one of these white rose bushes growing in our garden. It was a standard rose called Iceberg.

I strolled up to him and said I was going up to the cemetery and could I have the roses he was throwing into his bag. Well I walked away with a beautiful, very large bunch of white roses for my girls, roses that had been grown in our Prince Alfred Park. The park had played such a significant part in our lives, all those years ago.

Helen and Sherry arrived and we set off for Pinegrove. I had some silk flowers I had brought from home. My white roses and I also purchased more flowers from the shop at Pinegrove. The girls' grave looked well cared for even before we stared to give it a wash-down.

Sandy Cain had come some time before with Stephen and Helen to replace the rose bush that had died and some fresh pebbles had also been added. My friends wandered off to visit their relatives' grave. I sat there in that peaceful, rather beautiful setting looking at all the colourful flowers, reflecting on how 30 years before I had decided on this large six-grave plot. Oh, all the trouble I had about the cost of it, but I had my way. I have always been determined, and determined about this I was.

AFTERWORD

STEPHEN'S STORY

Stephen, my son-in-law, did not have an idyllic childhood or adolescent life. His father deserted the family when Stephen was 7 years old. When he was 3 years old his mother had sent him to live with his grandmother. After Stephen's father left he was again sent to his grandmother. Stephen resented being sent away and he held this against his mother all his life. In doing this she left a permanent ache in his heart. She had sent him to live with this old lady and he always felt she was too old to shape a young child's life in those formative years. Plus, he was to be separated from his siblings; he has always loved and respected his brother and sister. There has always been a special bond between them.

I always saw Stephen as an introverted, quiet person. However, one to one, he and I often talked throughout the whole night. Stephen is an intelligent and extremely knowledgeable young man. I have always felt I could go to him with a problem or a query and he had an answer or a theory.

Stephen never gave up on meeting his dad again. However,

he had turned 50 years of age before he had news of him and unfortunately his father, Leslie Ernest Cain, had passed away by this time.

I asked him one day, "Stephen, what would you do if you found your dad?"

He replied, "June, I need to ask him one question. Why did you leave?"

Stephen pondered all his life on Why? Why did he leave him?

Stephen's older brother is Leslie Cain and his sister's name is Cathy.

Stephen and I were at a Healthy Life conference in Melbourne one year and I asked him would we try and track his father down as Stephen had heard many years before that his dad was living in Melbourne. His answer was "Leave it alone, June!" Stephen was always a man of such few words I often was unsure what he was thinking.

About 6 years ago Stephen received a letter from a woman in Melbourne. This lady, her name was Sharon, had had a relationship with Stephen's stepbrother. She had had children by the half-brother and was trying to track their family heritage for her children.

Stephen made contact with this lady and managed to learn a great deal about his father's life. After his father left home he had lived not far from them for about three years in Blacktown. Les Cain Senior then went to Melbourne and formed a new life with a woman who had two children to him. His first child in this new relationship was a boy. Amazingly he called him Leslie as he had called his first child to Daphne, Stephen's mother.

So now we have three Leslie Cains. Leslie Senior, Leslie Cain junior, and yet another Leslie Cain.

Sharon still has contact with that family. As she wanted to know about her children's heritage she tracked down Stephen in Sydney by letter and so this incredible story unfolds.

When we were living in Doonside and Cathy was attending business college she met Stephen Cain. The Cain family also lived in Doonside, just a few streets away from us in this small semi-country town.

Cathy enchanted Stephen. Her beautiful long, blonde hair, big blue eyes and sparkling personality he found irresistible. She was always laughing, giggling. After she met Stephen she seemed to laugh all the time. The sound of her laughter rang through our home.

Years after Cathy died Stephen told me he believed it was an act of fate him meeting Cathy. Yes, she danced into his life and his heart. He said he found it inconceivable that such an intelligent, exuberant young girl could possibly fall in love with him. Stephen had never had very high self-esteem and he was just over the moon. "June," he said to me one day, "You could go through your whole life and never have such a thing happen to you as I have had, in meeting Cathy." Having had such as her to share such a short time. It could never happen again." But then, forever with Cathy would never have been long enough for Stephen!

After about 20 years I said to him one day, "Stephen, you must give up on looking for another Cathy! It is not going to happen. It is not fair to another girl. You need to find someone altogether different. There are some great young women out there." He looked at me with the saddest, most forlorn look in his eyes. He did not answer. He just looked away.

Cathy and Stephen lived in the house my dad had bought for us in Victoria Road, Parramatta after they were married. After the girls died I moved back into the house. My marriage was over and we both thought we would be fit company for each other. Reflecting back it was not such a good idea. We were both so terribly grief-stricken. Stephen's life was full of turmoil and misery.

I remember one night he was crying, almost sobbing. He was punching the wall in the dining room. Then he slumped on a chair sobbing. He said, "I feel so ashamed that I am sorry for myself. It is the girls' who lost their lives and I am so sad I am left without my Cathy."

Stephen hardly worked for years. He travelled Australia and then he travelled overseas, always with his stepbrother-in-law, Brian's son Steven.

I feel he kept travelling until he had spent all their money. Cathy was always such a saver. He could not settle. After a time I moved to Perth and he came over to me for a short time. He ended up staying for over a year.

My friend Betty Mitchell and I had reared our children together and had been friends for many years. She had two children, Ian and Vicki.

While staying with me, Stephen took Vicki Mitchell out a few times. Vicki is a strong young woman, however, nothing serious developed between them. They were just friends. I discovered only recently, after all these years while chatting to Vicki on the phone that something might have developed between them. Vicki was not unlike Cathy. Yes, Vicki told me she had often given the relationship, herself and Stephen, some thought. She said, "June, I couldn't go there. I felt I would be being disloyal to Cathy."

My heart ached… they would have been great together. Vicki married a man not unlike Stephen and she has had three children to him. What a difference that union would have made to all our lives…

Cathy was always saving for the future. Stephen came home on Friday nights and gave her his pay packet. Cathy gave him a portion and banked the remainder of Stephen's pay with her own wages.

Stephen always wanted a pool table. Cathy would not hear of such a waste of money as she saw it. After she died Stephen bought himself a pool table and it had a lot of use. He would have all his mates around in the evenings.

Life has dealt Stephen some cruel blows. He is such a good

person with very good principles. When he was leaving Perth to return to Sydney I said I would sell his car for him and send the money on. He decided he would give it to some friends of ours, Mike and Joy, as they badly needed a second car. He asked me to give it to them after he had left Perth. Stephen didn't expect any thanks. He has such a generous nature.

After he returned to Sydney he purchased a home at Pitt Town. I worried about him all the time. I often rang him on a Saturday evening and he was always home alone watching T.V. I would encourage him to get dressed and go to the club. He always said no, he was okay just having a quiet beer and watching TV. I felt he was leading such a wasted life for a young man who had such a lovely heart and so much to offer a young girl.

In the 1980s I was living in Queensland and I owned the Healthy Life shop in Carindale regional shopping centre. Stephen rented his house out and came up to live with me for three years. He started courting Sandy, who worked for me also. After the shop was sold Stephen returned to Sydney. Sandy went with him and they later married.

Stephen has a happy ending to his story. I believe he made a good choice in Sandy.

After more than 33 years Stephen still visits his Cathy's grave.

EPILOGUE

I am now in my twilight years.

Since going to NSW for the 30year memorial of the death of my girls at Granville I have moved house. I have moved away from the street where that horrific dog attack took place. Yes, I sold my beautiful home and moved to a totally new and hopefully safe environment. A place where Monet and I can walk safely and without fear.

Monet and I have made a new start. We look to the future.

I have always seen myself as a small tree, having such a fragile beginning. Being lovingly entrenched in the best possible soil fed with love and cared for. A tree nurtured from its fragility into a strong, healthy tree. My life has been like this tree, able to withstand the storms and hurricanes of life.

The book is finally finished. Thirty-three years have elapsed since the death of my girls.

Going back after many years was so difficult for me, so heart wrenching. My supreme inner strength came to the fore again. I am proud of myself, what I have accomplished in my life. I look to the future with peace and tranquillity walking beside me, holding my hand.

I am now living out the retiring years of my life alone, but for the companionship of my darling Monet. A life that should have been filled with visits and get togethers with children, grandchildren and even great-grandchildren.

People may wonder how does one move on with life in the face of such a terrible tragedy. Unfortunately, I have never found the answer in my personal journey since the 18th January, 1977.

The struggle, the aloneness, is always with me.

THEIR EPITAPH

Sisters, they travelled through life hand in hand.

Together they took God's hands and travelled on to a better land.

18 January 1977

Cathy Cain
11.6.1957-18.1.1977
19 Years

Lyndy Stiles
18.9.1958-18.1.1977
18 Years

Thirty odd years on, and the pain, it never goes away.

To outlive one child is the cruellest thing.

To outlive both is a life sentence.